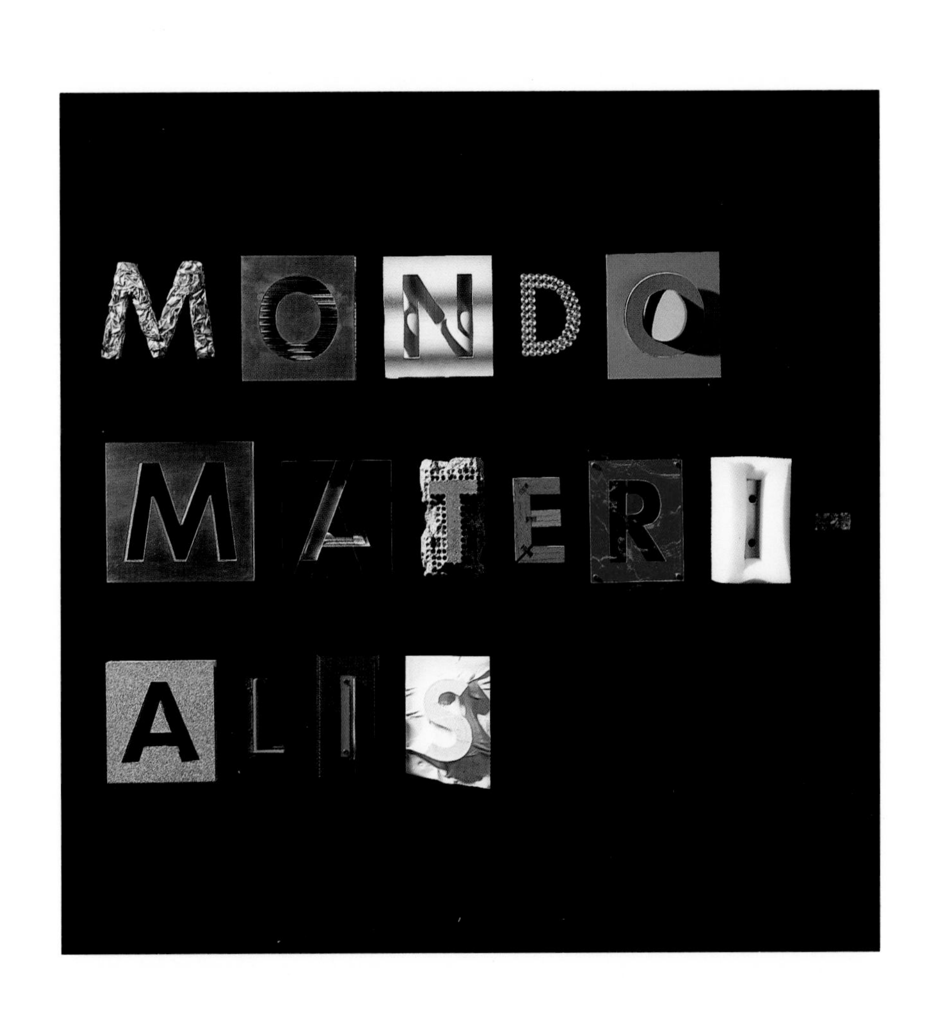
MONDO
MATERI-
ALIS

MONDO MATERIALIS

Crushed copper foil

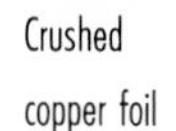

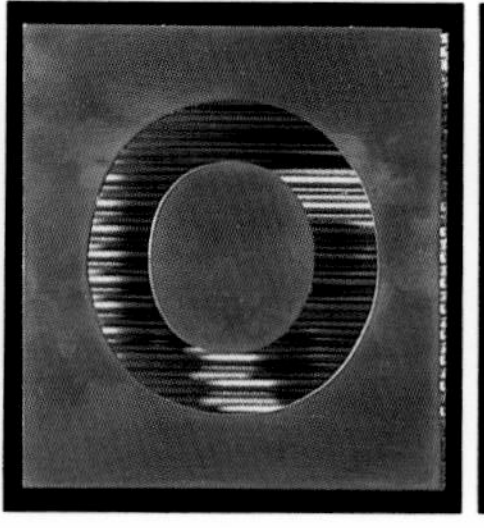

Aluminum sheet– natural; corrugated

Ash veneer– corrugated laminate

Aluminum rod with machined ends

High-density polyurethane from recycled milk jugs

Based on an exhibition created by **S***teelcase Design Partnership*

MATERIALS AND IDEAS FOR THE FUTURE

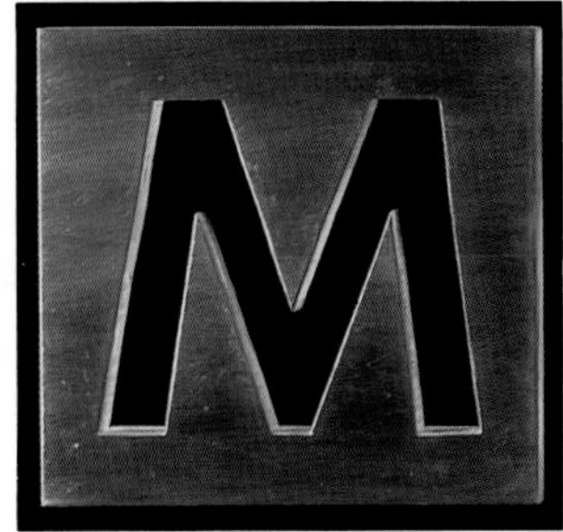

Brush-finished copper sheet laminated to acrylic

Blued aluminum with machined areas

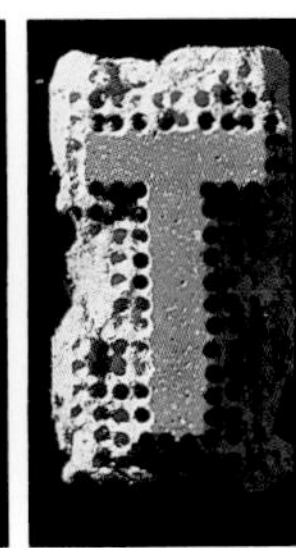

Syndecrete with background chipped and drilled

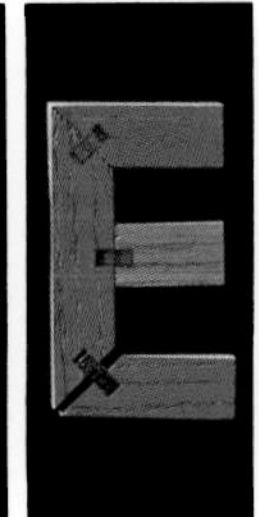

Aniline-dyed oak with aniline-dyed ash splines

Acrylic bolted to marble paper substrate glass

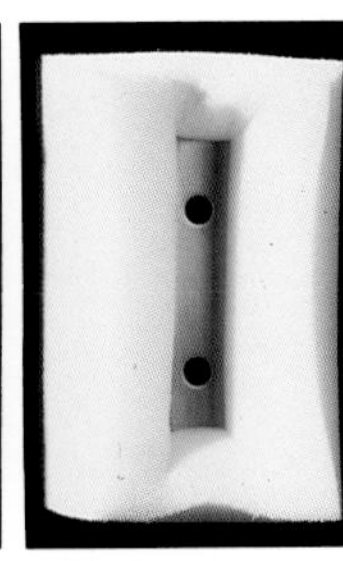

Brush-finished aluminum bolted to foam rubber

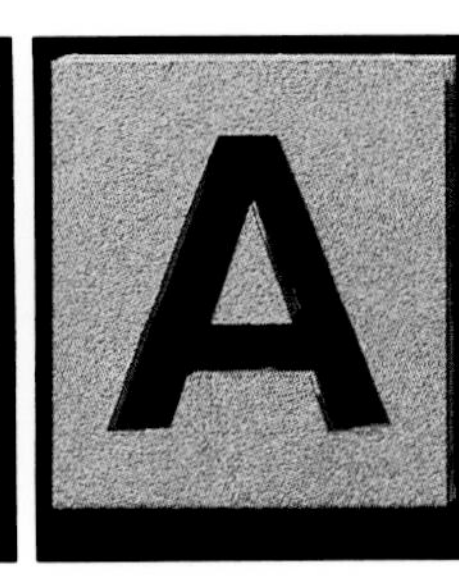

Smooth-finished sintered metal

Angle iron and fluorescent acrylic

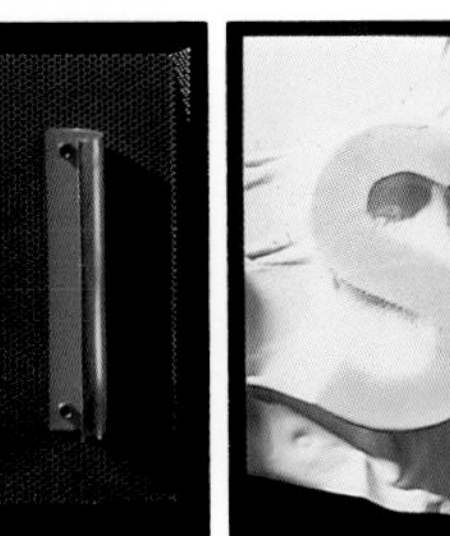

Tubing with brushed chrome exterior and acrylic-painted interior

Vacuum-formed matte-finish acetate sheet

By George M. Beylerian and Jeffrey J. Osborne

Photographs by Elliott Kaufman

Harry N. Abrams, Inc., Publishers, New York

Editor: Ruth A. Peltason
Designer: Samuel N. Antupit

The Steelcase Design Partnership is a group of leading contract furnishing, lighting, and textile companies: Atelier International, Brayton International, Design Tex, Details, Metropolitan Furniture, and Vecta. Under the aegis of Steelcase, Inc., the Steelcase Design Partnership has become a source of cultural inspiration for the architecture and design community.

Steelcase Design Partnership
305 East 63rd Street
New York, N.Y. 10021
(Phone) 212-755-6300
(Fax) 212-755-6309

Library of Congress Cataloging-in-Publication Data

Mondo materialis: materials and ideas for the future/introduction
by George M. Beylerian and Jeffrey J. Osborne.
p. cm.
"Based on an exhibition created by Steelcase Design Partnership."
Catalogue of an exhibition to be held at the Cooper-Hewitt Museum, New York City, which will travel through the country over the next 2 years.
ISBN 0-8109-3613-5
1. Architecture, Modern—20th century—Themes, motives—Exhibitions. 2. Design—History—20th century—Themes, motives—Exhibitions. I. Steelcase Design Partnership (New York, N.Y.) II. Cooper-Hewitt Museum.
NA680.M59 1990 90-547
745.4'442—dc20 CIP
ISBN 0–8109–2468–4 (pbk.)

Published in 1990 by Harry N. Abrams, Incorporated, New York. A Times Mirror Company.

Printed and bound in Japan

Page 1: Construction by Samuel N. Antupit and Porcelli Associates

Contents

Preface

ince the beginning of time, man has had an intimate relationship with materials, which has been based not only on admiration but by necessity.

As we approach the end of another millennium, we are able to celebrate enormous progress in new discoveries and developments through the catalyst of survival: *materials*. As we step outward into the universe of space, we seem to discover new materials, or maybe re-process or develop older materials at a geometrically expanding rate. The mystery of invention! If only we could unwind the thread from the spool to see what else will be discovered, achieved, and attained. Would this discovery make our lives more comfortable? More frenetic? Indeed, man has been haunted, challenged, and driven to exploit materials through the processes of extraction (mining, cutting of trees, etc.), transformation, and application.

Man, with his infinite mind, is master of his world of materials – those taken from nature, and those he has newly created; man also has the ability to achieve a harmonious balance of them in his environment. Technology can now provide new uses and new interpretations of nature's materials.

Nevertheless, as we accumulate new technology, many of civilization's older materials and processes seem to emerge, or to be perpetuated. Although the industrial revolution has changed the patterns of our life-styles, many elements, processes, and styles continue to mark our lives. Whether it's gold leaf, mosaics, terra cotta, frescoes or patinas, we continue to remember them all. Is it nostalgia or the simple appreciation of things beautiful?

The mere fact that museums exist proves that our civilization—man, instinctively—likes to keep and collect that which is considered beautiful. Over the centuries, artifacts come to represent the materials of their own era: clay, stone, marble, wood, canvas, and paint—mediums with which each era has expressed itself and reflected its zeitgeist.

Today, our art in museums is represented by "mixed media," material explorations, and conceptual art, ideas that transcend basic, given materials. Reflecting upon these mediums and processes, it is clear that artists have always been the forerunners of experimentation—they have set up their own R&D departments to fashion works that seem to express their current emotions, and their explorations of ideas and materials continue to point us toward the future.

These ideas have also found their way into the built environment through the special finishes, juxtapositions, or transformations that artists experiment with. As microchip technology now can mimic nature and surpass it, artists and designers are compulsively driven to counterbalance this movement by exploring, combining, and creating a plethora of artistic effects, producing a movement known as high-touch—obviously a reaction to the bare-bones materialism known as high-tech.

The materials presented in this book represent the ideas of 125 architects and designers of this decade, who have expressed their thoughts and feelings about the importance of materials in their work. They have expressed these ideas either through humor, juxtaposition, polemic presentation, or even through beautiful and sensitive designs, making statements using materials as products of nature, as products of invention or artificial intelligence, or by contrasts. In other words, the work represented here is a time capsule of this thinking process and of the state of the arts. By way of introducing this work, I wish to state that materials are the gateway of our civilization as they affect every phase of our life. Materials create inventions and inventions create products—products that we live in, live with, and use to make our lives better. And then, there are those materials provided by nature that we take for granted.

There are also materials that seem quite ordinary but become very precious when we process them or use them in a special way. A piece of blank paper may have little value, but information that we might put on it could give this paper enormous value. A "wall" in Berlin could be very ugly, oppressive, and detestable, but once it's demolished, fragments become historic relics and command enormous prices. This is the symbolic process of cultural or philosophical ad valorem. But how well does it illustrate the point when technical knowledge can also transform materials to become more precious? The object of this book is to record at a specific point in time the sensitivities and applications of materials through the artistic and stylistic representations made by the participants, together with their thoughts and concerns about specific issues.

Hopefully, this book will serve to broaden our sensibilities and awareness of materials, their sources and properties, and their capabilities to assume different shapes and functions. And lastly, *Mondo Materialis* is a visual reminder that we have to treasure our resources and yet look forward to materials of the future.

George M. Beylerian

Introduction

Material: the substance or substances of which a thing is made or composed; anything that serves as crude or raw material to be used or developed; any constituent element. (*Random House Dictionary of the English Language*. 2nd ed., unabridged, 1987)

Mondo Materialis is an exploration of materials in the built environment. The collage panels of materials included in this book were created by an international group of architects, interior designers, and product designers for inclusion in an exhibition sponsored by The Steelcase Design Partnership. Our intention in mounting the "Mondo Materialis" exhibition was to present an overall look at the next generation of design through the prism of materials. Our charge to invited participants was to "think of materials you find vital and fresh, whether they are traditional or new. These may include finishes, processes or textures which inspire you. We want to present a palette which you believe will be important in your work for the next five years. The panel you create should be in the most communicative form. What is desired is an artful collage of materials."

The panels assembled for "Mondo Materialis" tell us volumes about what materials are readily available for use by designers in the built environment and what materials are currently in vogue. They raise issues of social responsibility and environmental preservation. And they are, most certainly, artful. These presentations make us aware of the influence of fine art in the work of architects and designers and the importance of style and fashion in determining what materials are chosen for use in buildings and products.

Mondo Materialis is a beautiful celebration of materials and a time capsule that reflects the cultural and creative concerns of design professionals in the final decade of the twentieth century. It is interesting that, although some of the collages directly address new materials, most of the architects and designers who presented their ideas did not make their first priority the exploration of cutting-edge technology. There is innovation in the approach to materials here, but it is essentially innovation in context, in the way materials are used to define, enhance, reinforce, and reinterpret each other and to comment on our world. Perhaps this focus is a simple reflection of the current concern worldwide with the negative aspects of technology. But we suggest that it is related to several other factors as well. These include the nature of the process by which new materials are developed and enter mainstream design vocabulary; the changing role of the architect and designer in transforming and interpreting materials; and the educational process by which creative professionals learn about new materials and their possibilities.

Engineering: the art or science of making practical application of the knowledge of pure sciences, as physics and chemistry. (*Random House Dictionary*)

The development in our time of new materials, finishes, and processes applicable to the built environment is based upon sophisticated technology, a by-product of pure research. Through applied research, primarily materials engineering, such technology enters the realm of the usable. The advanced materials developed for use in specialized fields, such as space exploration, are eventually transformed into materials having wider, economical application, including the built environment. In general, architects and designers are dependent upon materials manufacturers for creating products they can use and for disseminating information about those products. But this is a lengthy and complex process, the success of which depends not only upon the quality of research but upon speculative investment and risk taking, which are not outstanding features of current business practice, especially in the United States.

Design for the built environment is thus limited by the pool of available and adaptable materials, which leads us to consider how extensive is this resource from which designers may choose, and whether there are materials outside the discipline of the built environment that have the potential to inspire innovation in design. While acknowledging the slowness with which new materials filter down into the marketplace, we believe that the world of material possibilities is larger than many architects and designers are aware of, and that the use of new materials, and the innovative application in the built environment of materials heretofore used in other industries or disciplines is limited by the failure of architecture and design schools, especially in the United States, to teach materials. Happily, the collages included here are evidence of the thoughtfulness, ingenuity, sophistication, and facility with which designers and architects use materials. It seems clear that the more information is given about potential resources, the more adventurous, and even richer, the designed environment can be.

hat do designers do
with the materials they select?

Design: describes the processes of selecting shapes, sizes, materials and colors to establish the form of something to be made. ... Sound relationships between the design process and the structure and materials of designed objects demand that the invention or selection of structure and the selection of structural and surface materials be an integral part of the process of design. (John F. Pile, *Design: Purpose, Form, and Meaning*. Univ. of Mass. Press, 1979)

Historically, the materials chosen by designers have been essential determinants of the forms of designed objects. Steel tubing was mass-produced and used in architectural railings (one of its first applications was in the Bauhaus school, where it was undoubtedly seen by Marcel Breuer and Mies van der Rohe), and the steam-bending of wood led to the design of wine barrels and, later, bentwood furniture. These developments were part of a design continuum in which formal and material invention built upon one another. The Modernist Movement was based on faith in that continuum. At its heart were the axioms that new materials led to new forms; that the evolution of new formal solutions was the essential work of design; and that structure and surface formed an integral whole. Modernism believed in functional efficiency, fitness for purpose, and truth to materials. It espoused volume rather than mass, regularity rather than symmetry, and dependence upon materials rather than upon applied ornament.

We no longer hold these truths to be self-evident. In 1966, Robert Venturi astounded the design world with the proposition that less is not more and that man could look to history for confirmation that diversity and variety, even complexity and contradiction, were signs of cultural and architectural richness. Venturi's *Complexity and Contradiction in Architecture* (1966) provided a manifesto for a new approach to materials and decoration. It offered a philosophic umbrella for the design community that espoused richness and ambiguity over unity and clarity, contradiction and redundancy over harmony and simplicity. In the 1980s, developments in materials technology created new vehicles for the expression of new cultural and material values.

Ezio Manzini, an Italian theorist of architectural engineering, analyzed the change in the impact of materials technology on our architecture and design in his book, *The Material of Invention* (1986):

After the Modern Movement culture rediscovered the value of surfaces and the sensory variables which surfaces can bear. By opposing the concrete and physical idea of of sensory quality to the abstract idea of formal quality, culture rehabilitated decoration, which modernism had branded immoral, and is now emphasizing the designer's control over the soft qualities of objects—not only visual qualities but also qualities of touch, warmth, smell. ... This many-faceted approach could not be understood overall if one were to ignore the simultaneous technical transformations that form its background, more or less unconsciously. The development of materials toward composites in which each layer has a specialized function sets the design and manufacturing problem of what qualities to give the outermost layer (the skin). The concept of a sincere image of materials thus becomes useless, in the way that the Modern Movement understood it. To the degree that materials have a skin their image is sincerely that of the skin, with the entire range of variations that the skin permits. ... Today the increasing spread of the artificial implies that the variety of surfaces has become a design topic, and that the surface quality is now determined for the most part independently of other formal and functional aspects. We are encountering, in short, the design of the relationship of closeness with objects.

In the 1990s new materials, such as lightweight metals and fabrics developed for use in space, and new processes, including those now revolutionizing glass technology, will lead to genuine formal invention in the built environment. And a cadre of industrial designers and architects working today, some of whose work is included in *Mondo Materialis*, steadfastly define design as the transformation of materials and dedicate their own energy to the exploration of new forms. But now, as we approach the twenty-first century, material invention that is immediately applicable to the built environment is concentrated on the proliferation of new surface finishes and materials. They provide a vast vocabulary for the expression of design ideas.

Metallurgical, ceramic, glass, and chemical engineering have given us a new palette of colors and textures in surface materials possessing functional properties such as light reflection and heat resistance as well as a disarming propensity for mimicry. Things are no longer what they seem. In architecture and design we have experienced the conceptual separation of materials and design process. Today we design buildings, interior spaces, and products upon which it is possible to impose an astounding variety of surface materials which bear little, if any, real or symbolic relationship to the structure of the materials they cover. The philosopher François Dagognet refers to this fundamental change as the "intellectualization" of materials and sees it as a liberating and creative force. "Materials and invention are becoming one," he exults. "Our imagination deserves to be freed of its stereotypes so that materiality can take free flight."

s we move away from a definition of design that postulates a direct correspondence between form and materials, two other concepts become important to our understanding of contemporary approaches to materials.

Art: the quality, production, expression or realm, according to aesthetic principles, of what is beautiful. *(Random House Dictionary)*

Fashion: a prevailing custom or style of dress, etiquette, socializing. ... Fashion, style, vogue imply popularity or widespread acceptance of manners, customs, dress, etc. *(Random House Dictionary)*

The artist, like the architect and designer, uses materials to explore ideas. The difference is in the artist's intention. He or she uses materials for purely subjective purposes while the designer works to fulfill a function and satisfy demands of the marketplace. (There are those who would argue that this distinction is no longer relevant given the advent of aggressive and carefully cultivated "markets" for fine art.) But the artist has played an important role in experimenting with new materials and devising forms, patterns, and juxtapositions of materials that are later appropriated by designers of the built environment. In this sense, artists are often the forerunners of design. Minimalist paintings predated minimalist interiors. In our time, artists possess the power to create fashion and it cannot be denied that fashionable elements, colors, and materials appear and reappear in the objects, façades, and interiors of the environments we build.

As we look at the 125 collages here that express our world of materials, we should recognize and place in perspective the roles that engineering, design, art, and fashion have played in the evolution of materials and in the education of those who use them to create the built environment.

There are several recurring themes expressed in the collages of *Mondo Materialis.* They provide insight into the ways that designers and architects define their own relationship to the material world at the beginning of this new decade. Some collages address more than one theme. For purposes of organization and clarity we have categorized each collage according to our perception of its dominant emphasis. We've identified seven themes, being Environmental Issues, Appropriateness of Materials, Essence of Materials: Artifice and Nature, New Technology/New Materials, Aesthetic Approaches, Juxtaposition of Materials, and Philosophical Reflections.

The environmental issues dealt with in the collages shown here include recycling, renewal, and the safe, efficient use of materials. The designers and architects who make these issues their first priority are highly conscious of the effects of their decisions and actions upon the environment. They include environmental impact as one of the central criteria for the selection of materials in their work. As such, they posit an active role for creators of the built environment in the survival of this planet. As knowledgeable users of materials and technology, they assume responsibility for protecting the environment from what is dangerous and for enhancing it through the use of renewable and recyclable resources.

The proponents of renewal advocate the use of natural materials, such as wood and animal skins, which are replenished by natural processes. But some take a wider view—"Remember nature" is their cry. Theirs is an admonishment to consider genuine needs, not just wants, in the creation of our built surroundings and to be aware of the effects of the processes of transformation, as well as the materials transformed, in the creation of building products.

The designers who call for recycling remind us that we must redefine our conception of "garbage." They reemploy existing materials by devising ingenious uses for what we have heretofore discarded, and discover ways to make new materials from those previously used. Some materials, they suggest, can actually be enriched by the recycling process.

Several participants address the issues of safety and efficiency in the use of materials. It is the responsibility of the designer and architect, they suggest, to apply materials in environmentally safe ways and to save resources by refusing to squander. In order to avoid waste, they advocate the use of standard materials in standard shapes and sizes and call for creative new applications of standard, economical, and plentiful materials.

The Appropriateness of Materials is the second theme that informs the work of *Mondo Materialis* contributors. This theme, which has been a leitmotif of modernist design, proposes that the selection of materials for use in creating objects and environments should derive, first and foremost, from a consideration of the properties of those materials in relation to the problems to be solved. Insofar as design involves a balance of function, price, and aesthetics in its search for solutions, the choice of appropriate materials in any given situation is a complex, many-sided issue. A few of the collages that focus on appropriateness show specific materials in specific applications. Some suggest the appropriateness of materials usually associated with one area of design to application in another. Others introduce new materials (paints, finishes, fabrics) developed as appropriate solutions for products in the built environment and still others assume the larger problem of orchestrating an appropriate admixture of many materials, each serving its purpose, to create total, harmonious environments.

The Essence of Materials: Artifice and Nature speaks to the essence, or value, inherent in materials. The designers and architects who created collages on this theme call out the material qualities that inspire them: truth, rhythm, perception, coherence, levity, sensibility, harmony. They point to the multiple lives that materials have, before and after their transformation by man, and the mystery at the heart of materials. The collages on this theme also question our traditional assumptions about the essential qualities of materials and make the observation that things are not always what they seem. Man-made materials, which have taken the place of natural materials in virtually every area of design, are based on artifice or ingenuity. The reality of such materials lies below the surface in the composites and alloys of which they are constructed. We cover them with thin veneers of natural materials in an effort to hide their essences and make them appear to be something that they are not. Which is real—the substance or the surface? One collage on this theme calls the material it presents "cultured wood," a reference to our ability to create natural/unnatural materials. These collages point to the way in which artifice follows nature and becomes so much a part of our given world that nature appears to imitate artifice.

Another thematic approach uniting many of the collages in this collection is a purely aesthetic approach to materials. The collages in this group make statements about what, and in what ways, materials may be used to produce calculated visual and tactile effects in the built environment. Some of them are based on nostalgia and romance, some on what we call a traditional modernist perspective, and others focus on the properties of surface and texture.

The collages that refer to nostalgia and romance tend to assume a decorative attitude. They are concerned with evocation—the summoning of comfort, tranquility, whimsy, and with imitation—the mimicry and restoration of materials of the past. Traditional materials and techniques, such as mosaics, evoke specific historical periods and styles. Found materials romanticize personal, serendipitous environments. The collages that express a traditional modernist perspective investigate "classic" materials, such as bronze, steel, brass, glass, and natural fibers. They refer to the elegance of materials and the integration of the aesthetic of the material with architecture. They seek to express the purity and clarity of materials. They exalt perfection, singularity, strength, and simplicity.

Several architects and designers emphasize the physical properties of surfaces and textures in their collages. They refer, in their written statements, to the emergence of surface and texture as the determinants of design in our decade, taking over the role played by color and form in decades prior to our own. They posit surface phenomena as new building materials with the power to activate the senses. These collages celebrate a tactile, sensory approach to environments and welcome new technologies that make the selection and mixing of finishes an important art in the creation of built environments.

The theme of juxtaposition, which threads its way through many of the *Mondo Materialis* collages, is about contrasting ideas, about putting opposites side by side, and about examining the relationships between materials. The collages in this group are concerned with the variability and diversity in materials and, by extension, the variability and diversity of the environments in which they are used. We believe that the popularity of juxtaposition as a theme, both in the exhibition and in the work of design professionals, is based on the continuing interest of designers and architects in exploring complexity and contradiction, ambiguity, and even perversity, in the built environment. These collages juxtapose natural and man-made, hard and soft, light and dark, the abstract and the concrete, the simple and the complex, common and precious, rough and smooth, old and new, fragile and tough, the transparent and the massive, the prosaic and the poetic. They make a place for a diversity of materials and meanings. They declare that through materials the built environment can reflect the full range of history, values, and aspirations of the culture it serves.

The fourth theme expressed is New Technology/New Materials. The creators of these collages explore new materials, products, and processes that they believe offer significant innovation for the built environment. They express technology, which is often invisible, and claim it as a benefit and a symbol of our time. They propose building methods based on ancient crafts, such as boat-building and tent-making, married to new, lightweight materials of great endurance and tensile strength. They present very old materials in new forms—and new materials that serve traditional purposes. They introduce electronic processes and devices that possess the ephemeral capacity to bring built environments to life. They pose the question of value: Do we reevaluate materials we have judged common, even vulgar, when innovations in their properties and the processes by which they are transformed give them new utility and new power to contribute to our environment?

Finally, a whole group of collages represents philosophical reflections on the meaning, implications, and uses of materials. Some are musings on history: They describe fresh winds from the East breathing new life into a dying Western civilization. They define our time as one characterized by "unbuilding" and chaos, a time in which we redefine the relationships between nature, man, and the built environment and so invent environments that can grow and change. They announce that the ancient borders have been destroyed, requiring a search for new forms, new boundaries. They declare that we already possess the materials of the future, and that their mastery comes via technology. Some speak of meaning and use: They find the meaning of materials not in technology, but in the intention of the architect or designer who transforms them. They reject the notion of a unifying philosophy of design for our time, and demand that our decisions about materials be based on more immediate, humane considerations. They argue that the meaning of materials awaits the imposition of form—design demands a "poetics of substance." They look for meaning in the unexpected, trusting in the "magic" of materials. They delight in the mythical and poetical uses of materials. They call for a surreal appraisal of materials that would lead to their use to express reality as it is, however shocking that might be.

The collages of *Mondo Materialis* provide a vision of what is possible and a sense of how designers, given perfect freedom, would choose materials. But the design of the built environment is carried out in the real world, where the freedom to create is limited by cost and culture. Materials have status and value. As Herbert Gans theorized, high culture, often through the medium of fine art, confers status on materials (and also on objects, clothing, and so forth), rendering them desirable and placing them in demand. After a time, popular culture adopts high culture's objects of desire and, in so doing, lessens their appeal to the elitist culture that crowned them. An object or material is rarely in vogue simultaneously in both cultural spheres. The balance between high culture and popular culture may swing back and forth many times in the life of a particular material or object, with designers often caught in the flow. They are drawn to high-status materials by their position in the social order and by their clients. Culture, not only technology, defines the materials they use in their work.

At the same time, cost is a factor in determining the materials with which architects and designers work. The bottom line has created a demand for materials that look rich but cost little, a need satisfied by new composite materials and surfacing technologies. The burden of responsibility falls on the manufacturer of materials to continue the search for such high-yield materials, balancing the short-term gains to be realized by producing tried technology against the long-term gains, both economical and ecological, to be achieved by aggressive materials research and engineering.

As materials choices become more complex, the burden falls upon the designer not only to enjoy the bounty of these benefits, but to understand and exploit their complexity. Design requires context and parameters, and the advancement of design requires knowledge of previous solutions. The mastery of materials must be a vital dimension of the work of architects and designers if the discipline of design is to advance. Design leadership consists in the wit to discern a need—and the ability to fill it with imagination. Materials are the tools of the imagination.

We live and work in a time that exalts individual expression and uniqueness. The collages included in this book are a cross section of creative personal expression. They celebrate a diversity of approaches and ideas. They highlight the artfulness of materials themselves and demonstrate a growing reciprocation and overlaying of design, art, and invention. They force us to consider the implications of a vastly expanding pool of materials, technologies, and processes coupled with a pluralistic attitude toward a theory of design. Anything *is* possible. The weight falls on the individual designer and architect to use expanding resources and expressive freedom productively—and responsibly.

Jeffrey J. Osborne

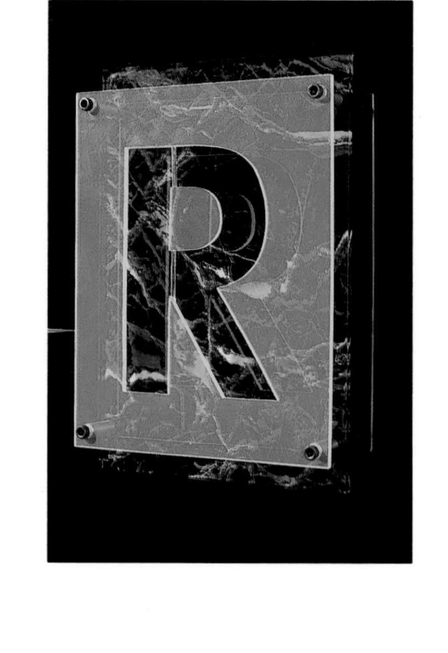

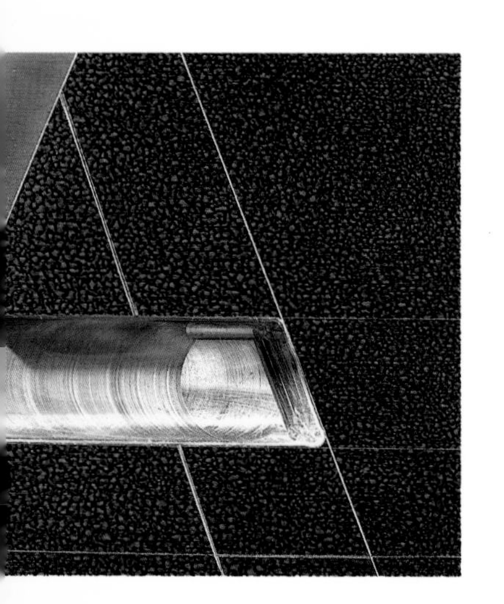

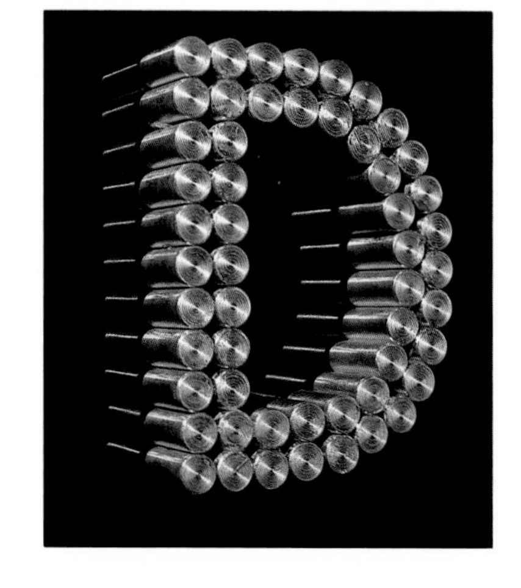

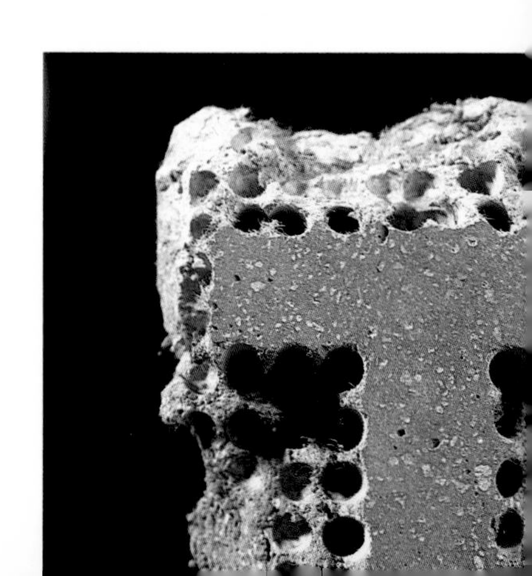

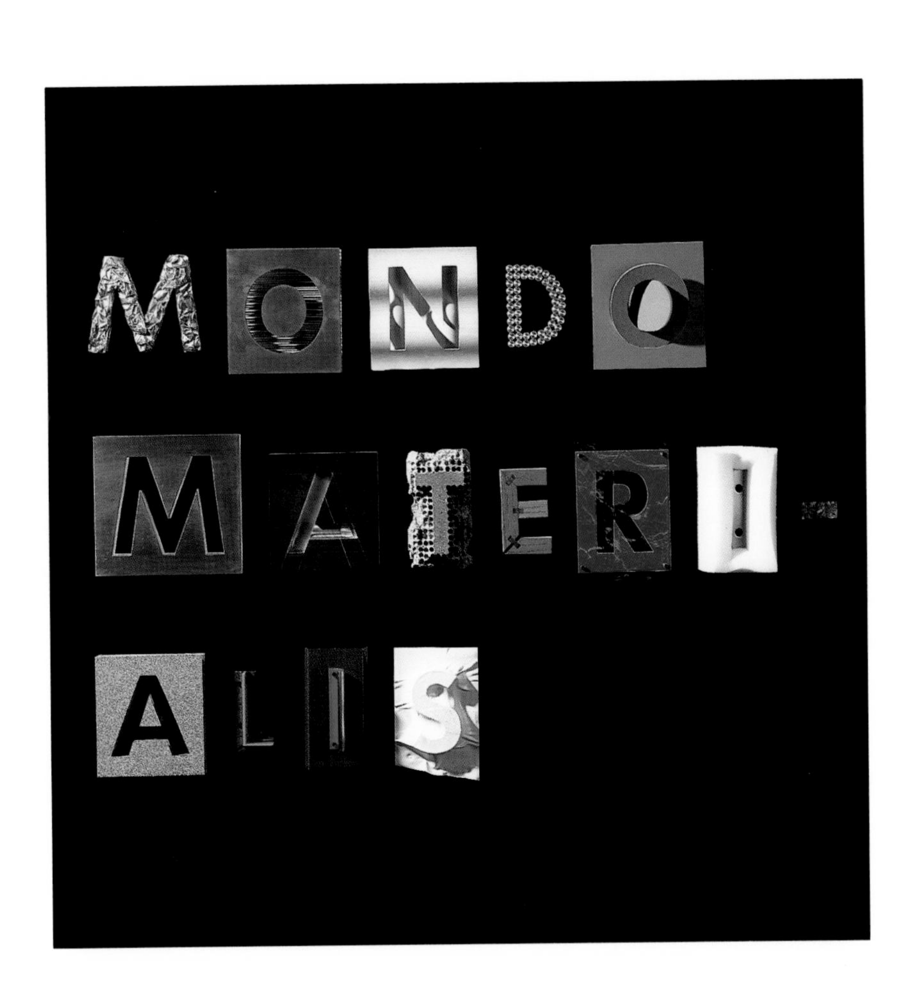
MONDO
MATERI-
ALIS

TORSTEN A. FRITZE

SAN FRANCISCO

Silver-coated cardboard, foamcore, ABS 0-3 sheets, styrene clear, Chinese (kang pao) leaves, gold leaf paper

"...soft, man-made aspects... are going to be the key element in the environment of the 90s. By 'soft aspect' I intend the intelligent use of light and printed materials, laminates in combination with traditional materials to enrich the environment."

MICHAEL SORKIN
NEW YORK

Asbestos

CONTAINS
ASBESTOS

WEBER & KALMES

LUXEMBOURG

Claude Kalmes,

Jean-Marie Weber

Metalized copper,

liquid oxidation agent,

solar light source,

sandblasted Douglas fir

"... we are always searching
for combinations
of old and new materials
to create a new dimension
having properties that cannot
otherwise be obtained
using just one of the components."

STUDIO SOWDEN

MILAN

George Sowden

Leaves

HELSINKI

Antti A. Nurmesniemi

Routed laminated pine

PAOLO PORTOGHESI ED ASSOCIATI

ROME

Paolo Portoghesi

Travertine marble frame, marble tiles, leaded glass, parquet floor

"It is only right and proper that traditional materials should come back into our homes to symbolize solidity and durability . . . to bring into the home the image of nature and its endless variety. What indeed could be better than the veining of a fine piece of stone to recall the beauty of a landscape . . . ?"

MICHAEL McDONOUGH, ARCHITECT

NEW YORK

Michael McDonough

Cardboard, aluminum cans,

vinyl adhesive caulk

*"**T**he panel... points to issues traditionally perceived as "outside of design"; that is, apart from important components of professional practice and materials technology for the 1990s. Its aluminum soda cans, cardboard, and vinyl adhesive caulk... are also reminders of solid waste, environmental, and other similar problems that will have continuing impact on design in the future."*

SMART DESIGN, INC.

NEW YORK

Tucker Viemeister, Peter Stathis, Jeanni Gerth, Rick Vermeulen

Brown glass, polyethylene, milk jugs, beer cans, credit cards, automobile trim, lint, newsprint, car window

"Today designers are positioned to play a vital role in the survival of the human race — indeed, of the whole planet. . . . We can no longer afford to throw anything away. The world is not going to get better until designers create sound products that consumers not only should use but want to use."

WOOD/MARSH

E. MELBOURNE, AUSTRALIA

Roger Wood, Randal Marsh

Recycled plastic, chrome, steel,

lacquered wood, particle board

"All these materials are precariously balanced between the environment and the future."

McCOY & McCOY

BLOOMFIELD HILLS, MICHIGAN

Michael and Katherine McCoy

Chopped foam

"Chopped foam is the material of the future with a past... the very embodiment of recycling, of taking cast-offs and making from them something new. It is one material that is enriched by the recycling process."

PADRÓS/RIART/TIÓ MOBLES CASAS

BARCELONA

Carlos Riart LLOP

Cow leather, sheep fur, gazelle fur, bamboo cane, hemp string

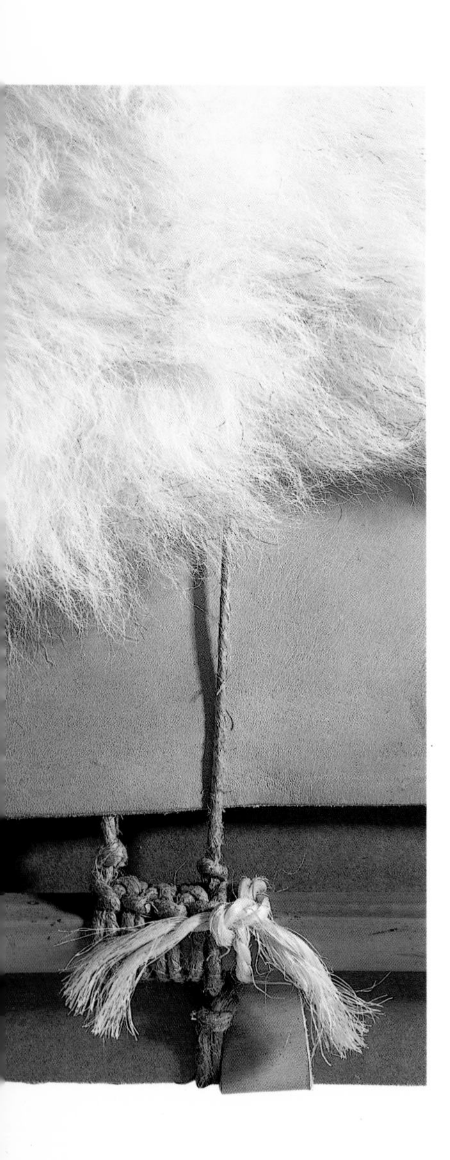

"I believe that technological advances should be focused upon regenerating what has been bequeathed to us. . . ."

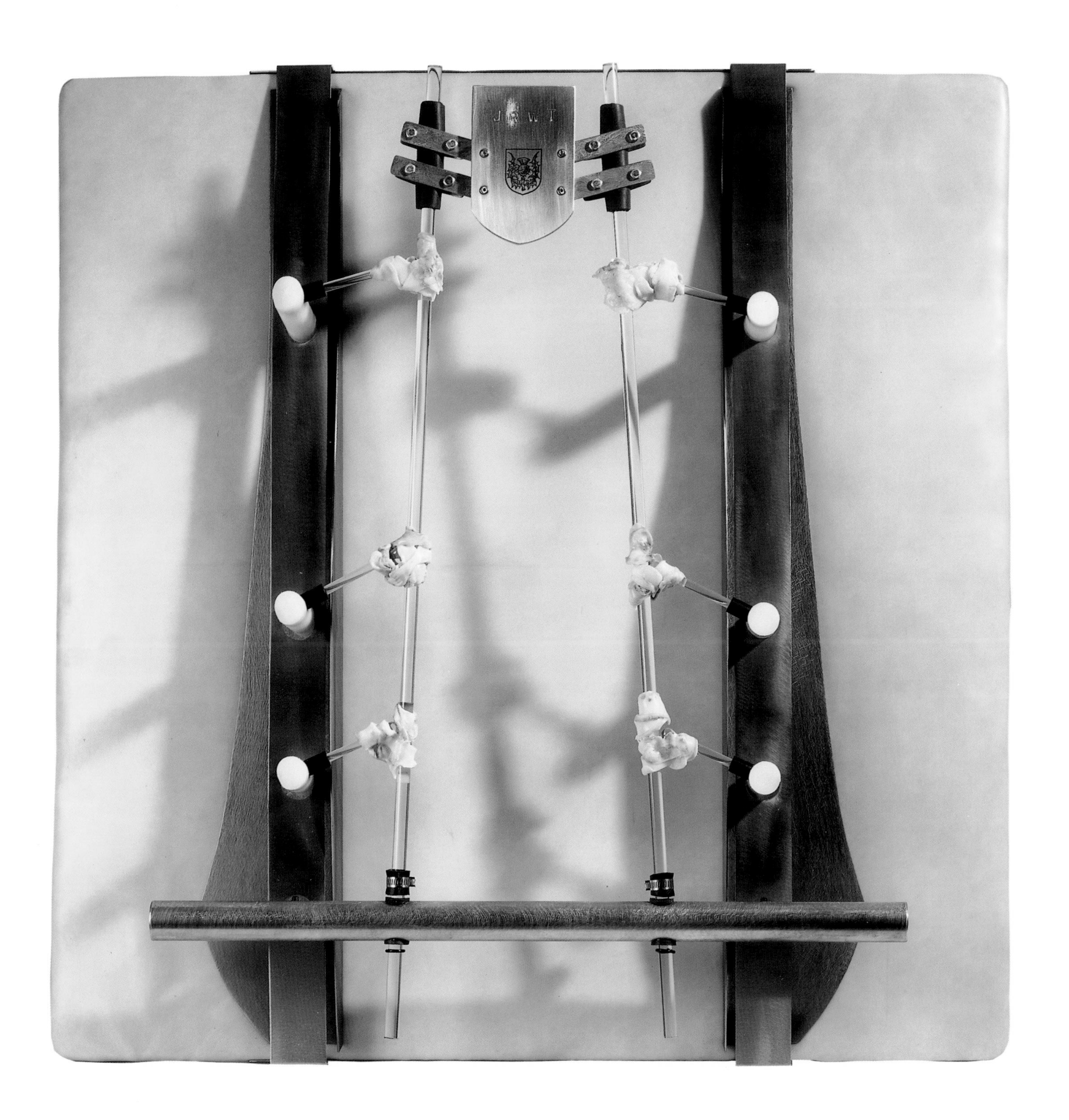

JONATHAN R.W. TEASDALE

NEW YORK

Steel, aluminum, glass, latex, neoprene, polyester, polyethylene, stainless steel

APPROPRIATENESS OF MATERIALS

MASAYUKI KUROKAWA ARCHITECT & ASSOCIATES

TOKYO

Masayuki Kurokawa

Titanium, aluminum,

stainless steel, lead, bronze,

rubber, zinc, glass

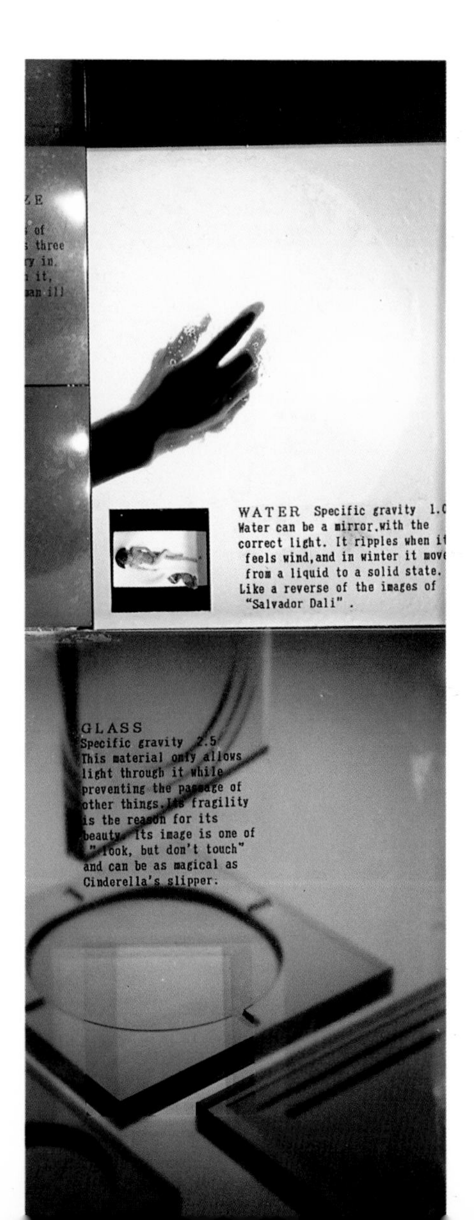

METROPOLITAN FURNITURE CORPORATION

SOUTH SAN FRANCISCO

Robert Arko

Embossed sanded leather, reconstituted wood, linoleum tile, electronic components, drill bit, floppy disk, found objects, metal bracket, oriented strandboard

"Due to resource, environmental, and related economic issues, natural materials are becoming increasingly elitist in application. More cost efficient man-made or man-modified material solutions are now used as substitutions and will play an ever-increasing role in years to come."

EVA JIRICNA ARCHITECTS

LONDON

Stainless steel, extruded aluminum — stair riser, laminate glass/silicone, rubberized cork, pressed metals, epoxy resin, sandstone, cherry veneer — stained and lacquered

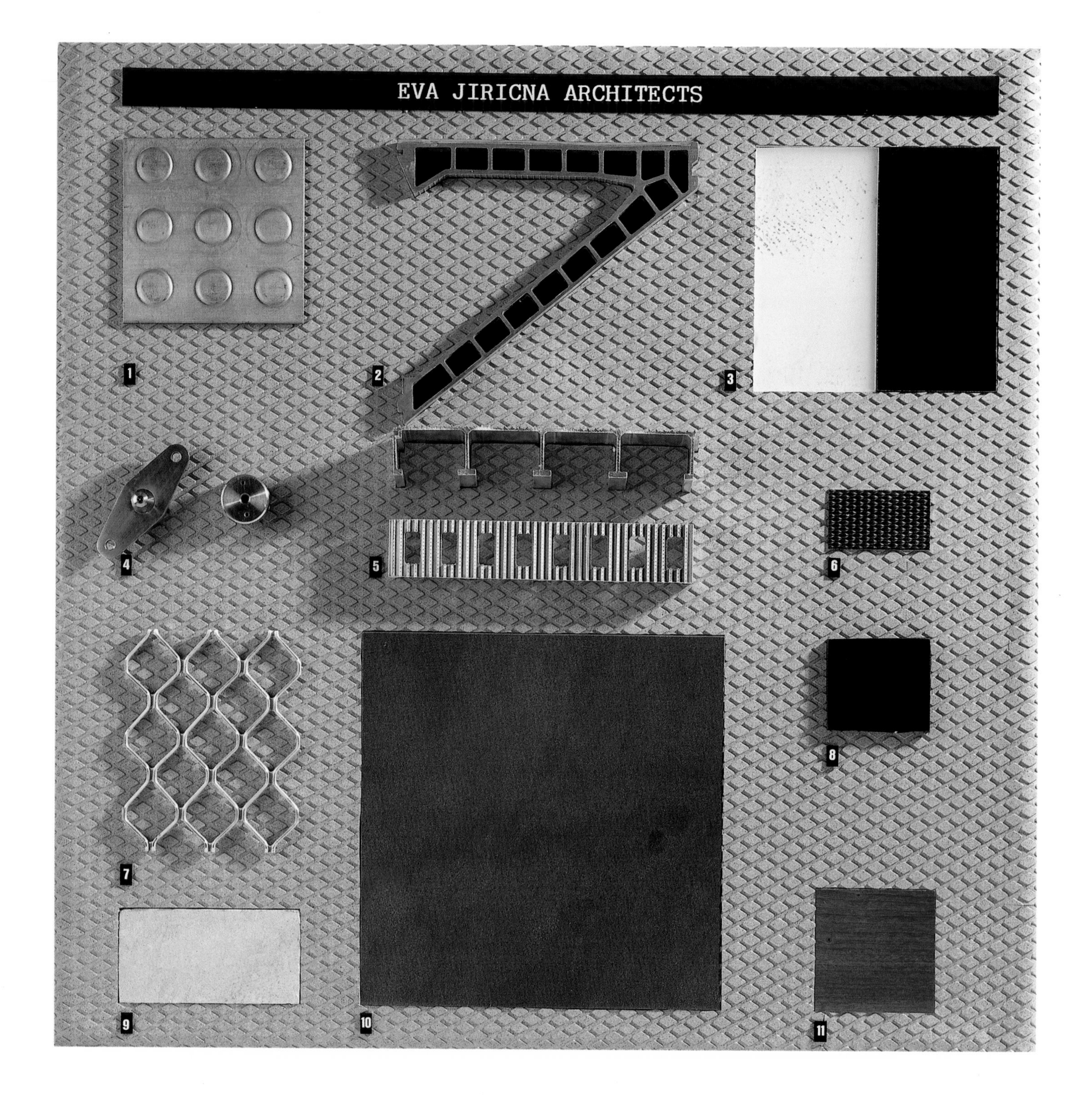

"Hopefully research programs, industrial production, and imagination will work more in conjunction so that materials can be used in a sensible and creative fashion, with due consideration to function, quality of life, economy, and conservation."

TOM McHUGH

PHILADELPHIA

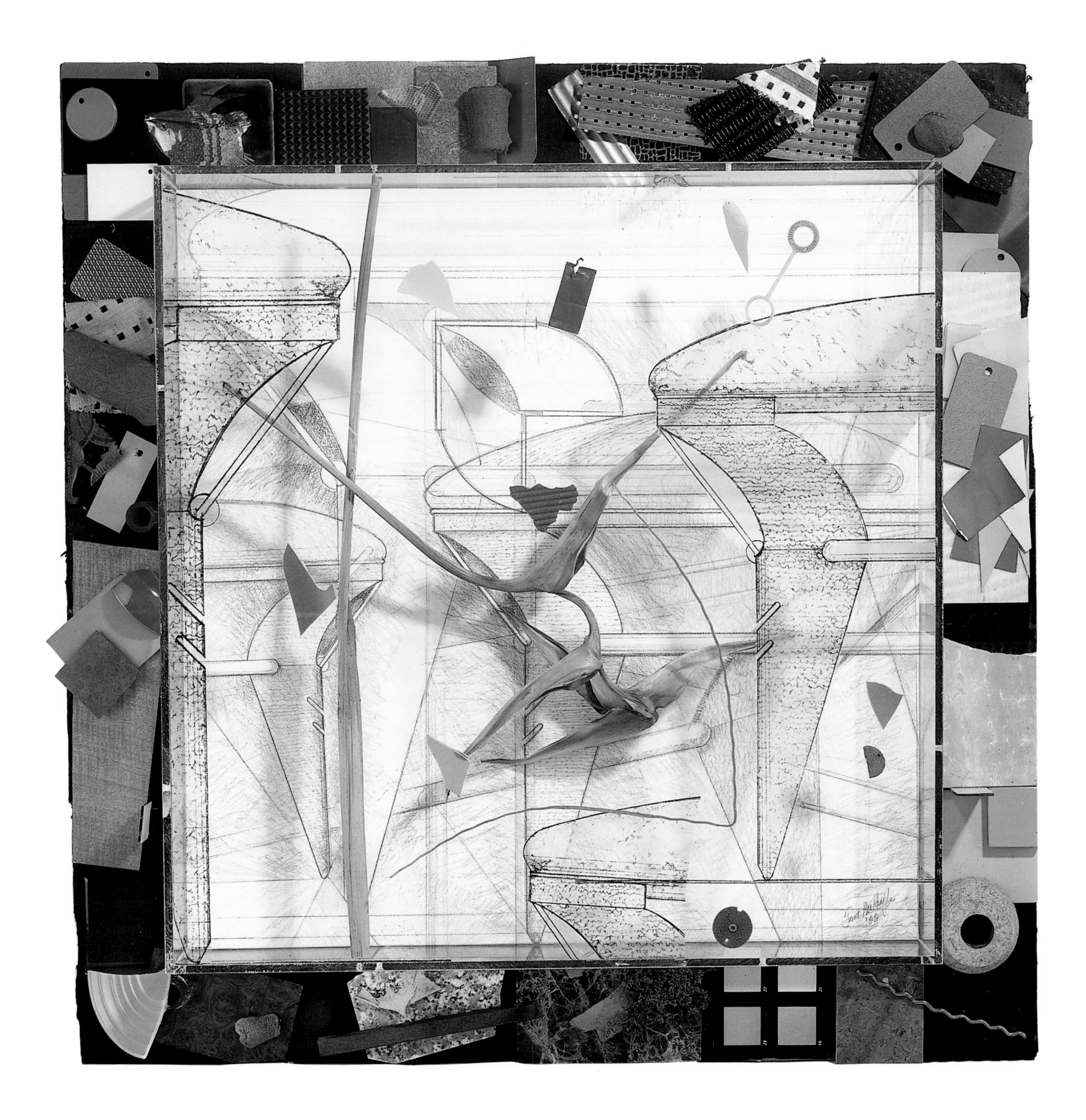

Fabric, glass, metal, stone, wood (tiger maple, anigre, elm burl), laminate, paint, linoleum

"In the nineties, economic conditions in the real estate market will result in much smaller rentable spaces, forcing designers to stretch the visual limits of these spaces. Also, with the advent of electrical components in advanced technology, it will be necessary to counterbalance these spaces with more personal visual anchors."

MURPHY/JAHN

CHICAGO

Nada Andric

Stainless steel with baked enamel, carpeting, fritted glass, etched, brushed, and enameled stainless steel

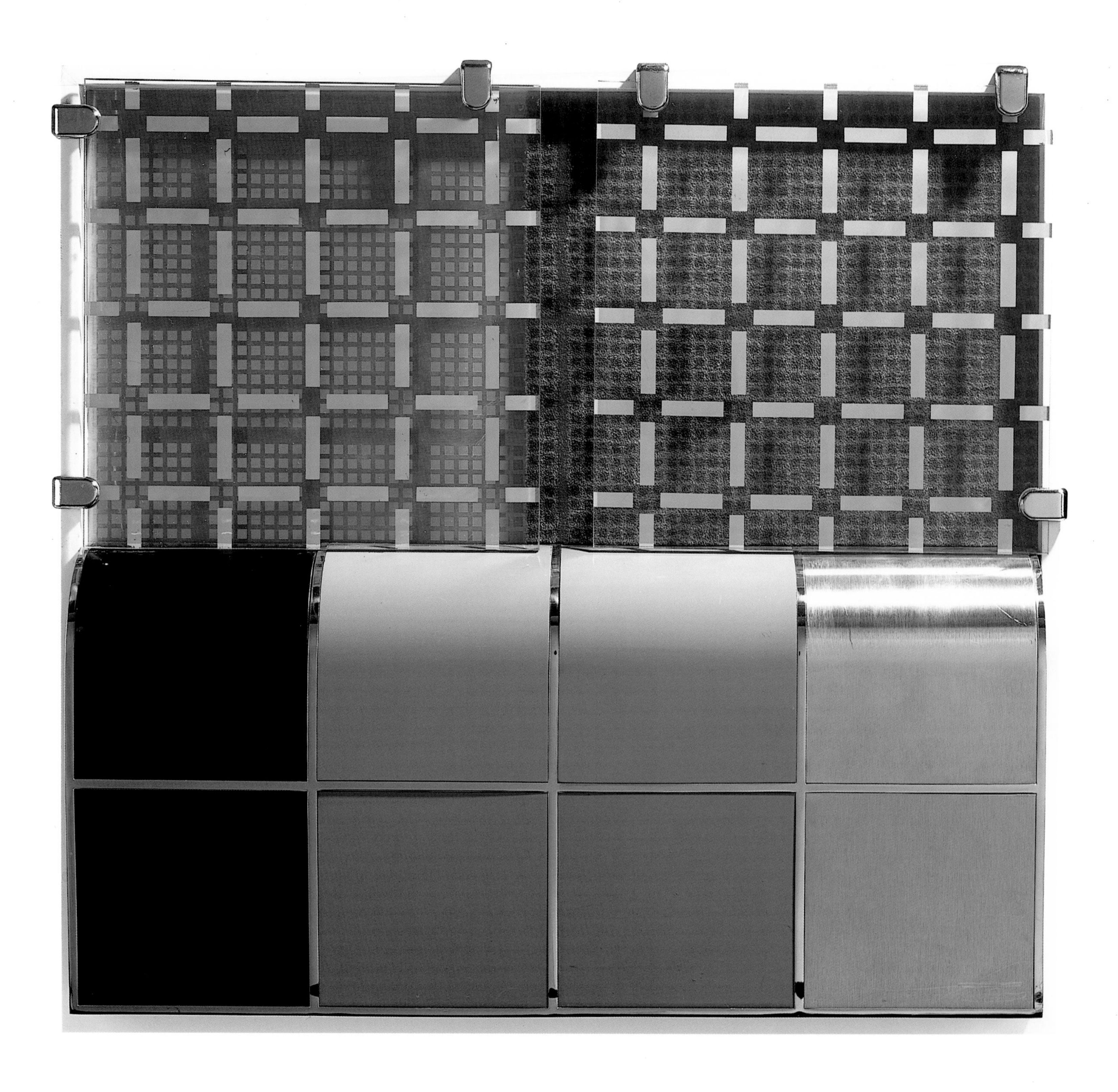

SUMFORM

LONG ISLAND CITY, NEW YORK

William Schiffman

Graphite, paper, foam, wood, rubber, steel, brass, cement, plastic, copper, aluminum, glass, silicone, sand, stone

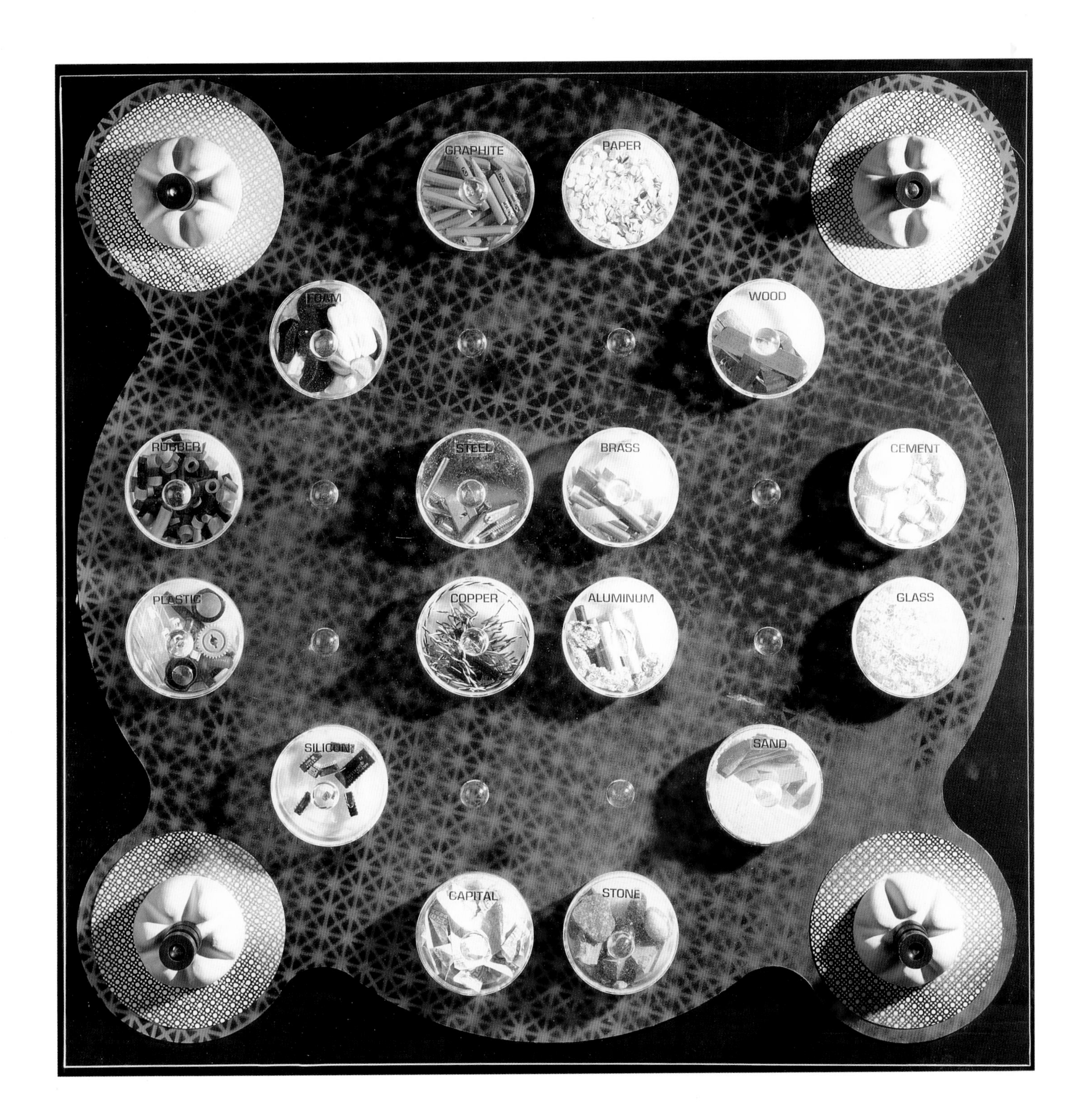

KAWAKAMI DESIGN ROOM

TOKYO

Motomi Kawakami

CFRP (carbon fiber reinforced plastic), titanium, continuous aramid filament yarn, stainless steel and steel (various finishes), melamine resins, rice paper, glass, stone, ceramic, printed metals, wood veneers, plastics, elastomeric monofilament fiber

DAVID ZELMAN

NEW YORK

Cardboard, steel, stainless steel

"... most of my work is inspired by the machine and other technological advances of the industrial age."

STUDIO DE LUCCHI

MILAN

Michele De Lucchi

Plastic laminate marquetry

"Now that there is much sensitivity concerning the safeguarding of nature, attempts will be made to understand whether it is better to use plastics and to control their uses and abuses, or to use natural materials and try to avoid their abuse."

COOP HIMMELBLAU VIENNA/ LOS ANGELES

WEST LOS ANGELES

Wolf D. Prix,

H. Swiczinsky

Foam insulation, steel, glass

STEELCASE INC.

GRAND RAPIDS, MICHIGAN

Colette Omans, Steelcase Industrial Design Group; Terence D. West, Industrial Design Director

Textured paint, metallic powder coatings, nylon in epoxy powdered coating, UV cured surface, fabrics, printed metals

ROSS LOVEGROVE

LONDON

Stainless steel nautical rope guide,

industrial ceramic, razor caps,

razor foil, rawl plugs,

disk camera film cassette,

computer chip,

heavy saddle leather, vinyls,

anodized aluminum board

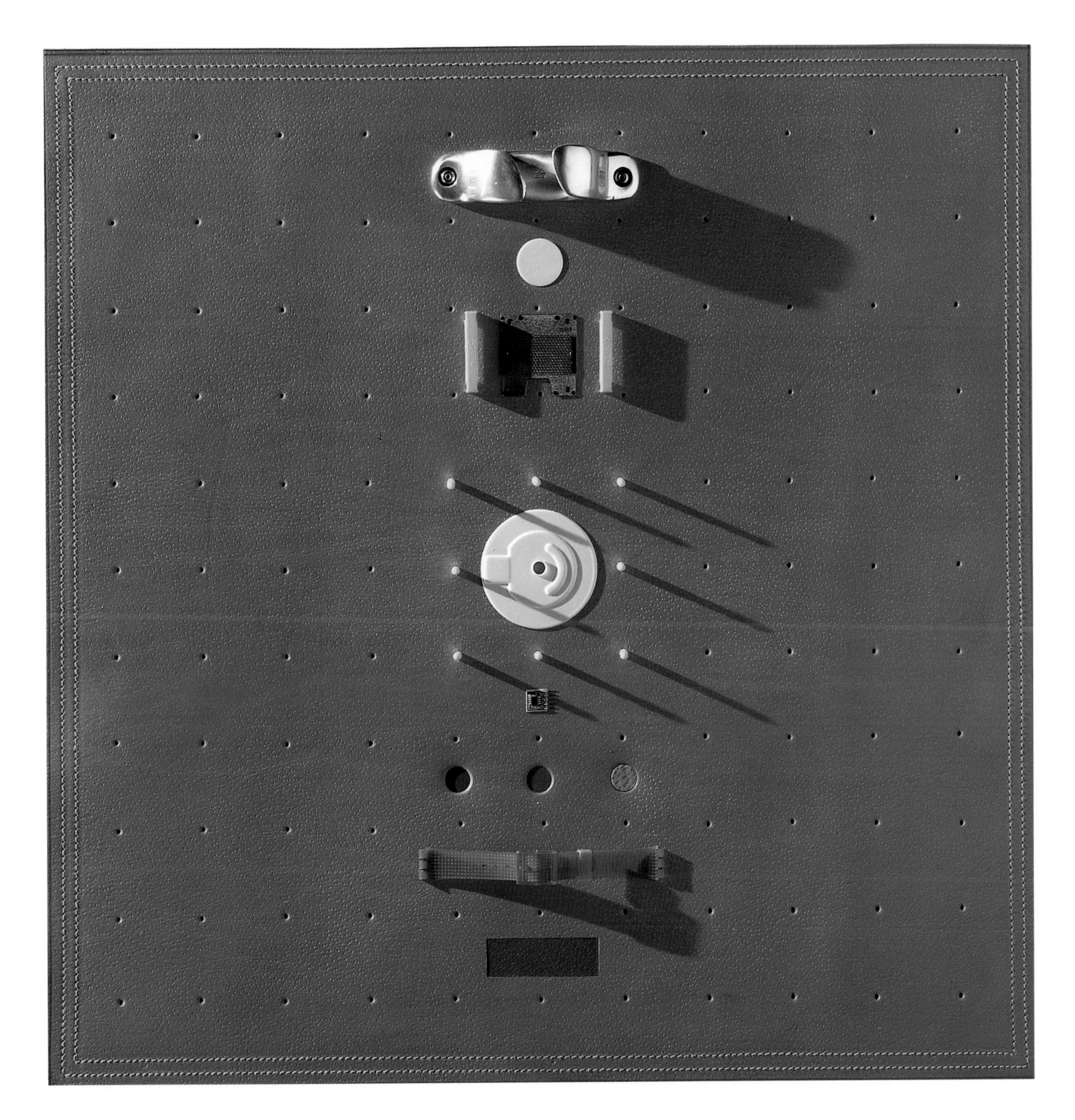

"In the way that a beautiful piece of architecture
needs a landscape or a setting
to express its true character,
small volumes of material...
require a deeper perspective
and a more valuable examination
rather than being tossed away as obsolete
or as infinitely replenishable."

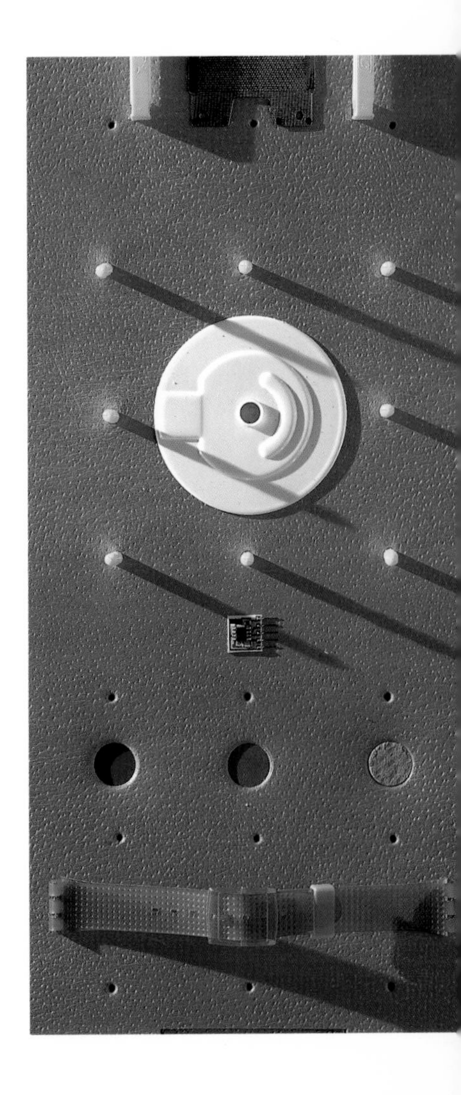

THE RICHARD PENNEY GROUP

NEW YORK

Richard Penney, Erica Pritchard, Frank Young

Cold-rolled steel, hot-rolled steel, aluminum paint on Dryvit, sandblasted cold-rolled steel, etched pewter, cherry wood, sandblasted mirror, hand-drawn textile, wood solids

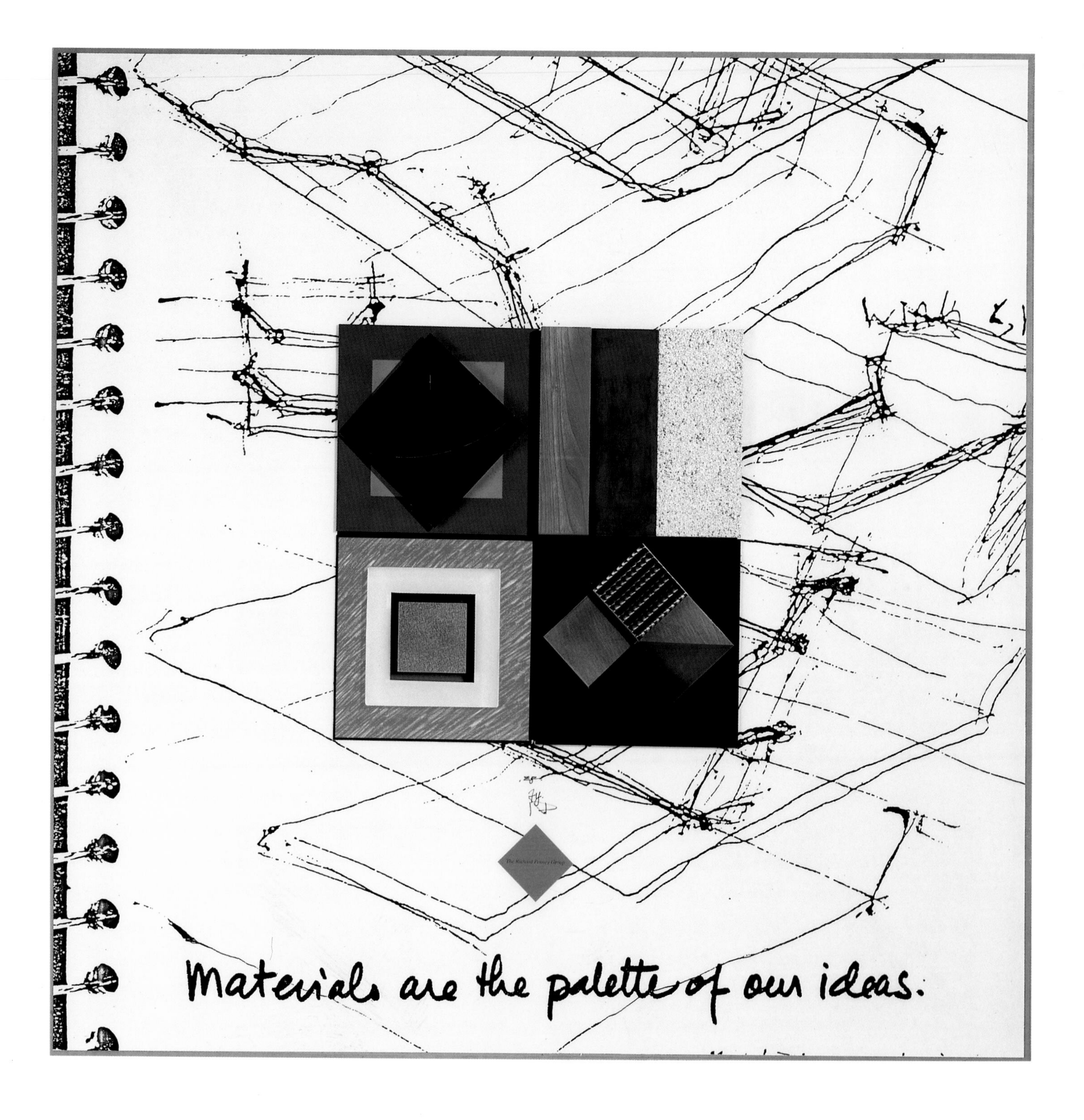

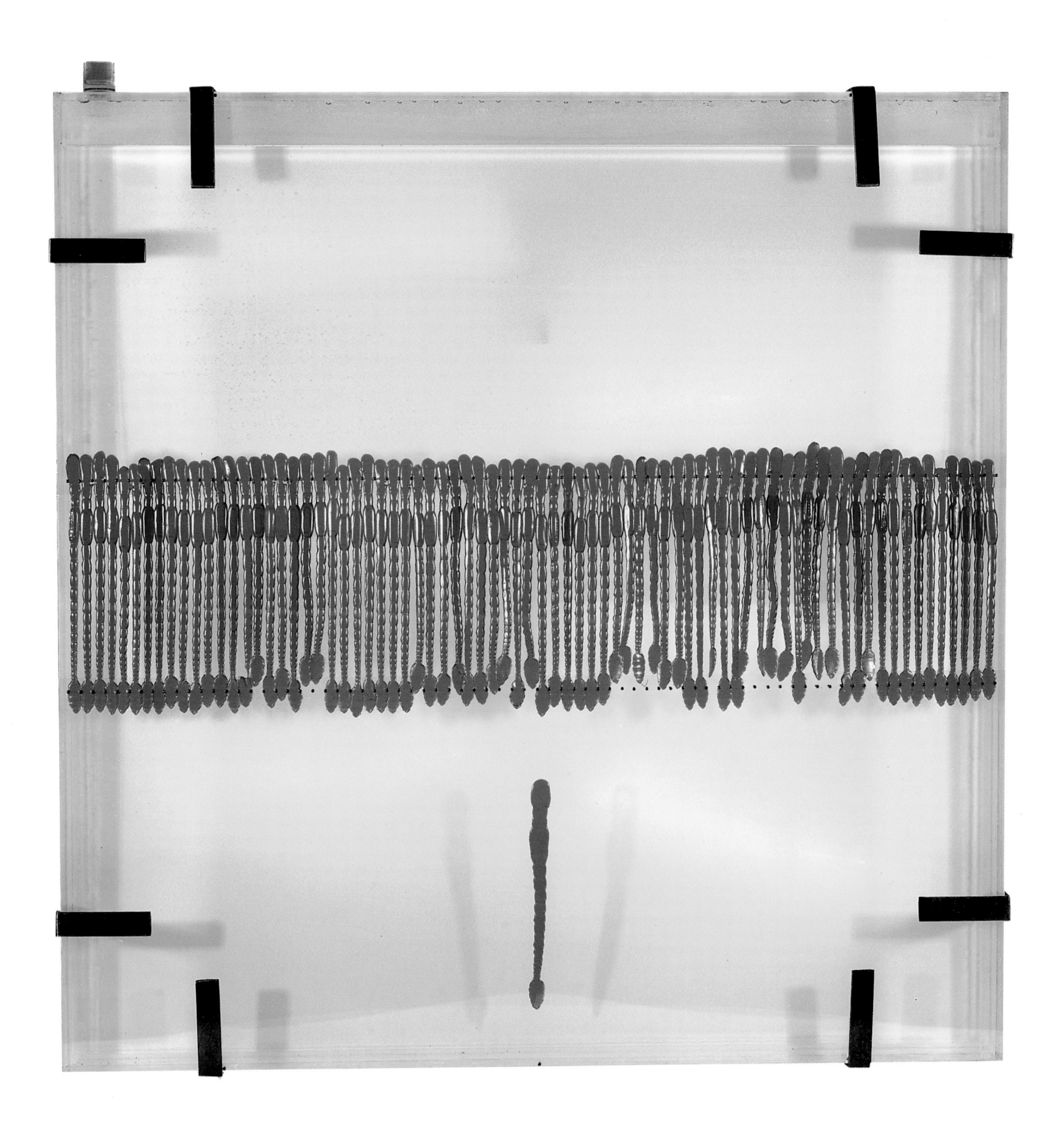

ABLE

NEW YORK

Lisa Krohn, Martha Davis

Water, fishing lures,

synthetic rubber worms,

Plexiglas, foil,

electrical connectors,

metal strapping

WALZ DESIGN

NEW YORK

Kevin Walz

Athletic flooring, galvanized metal, sandpaper, lacrosse ball, rubber chipboard, shearling, soil-erosion matting, blackened steel, belting leather, textured plastic, acoustical material, rubber, fiberglass, copper mesh, cork

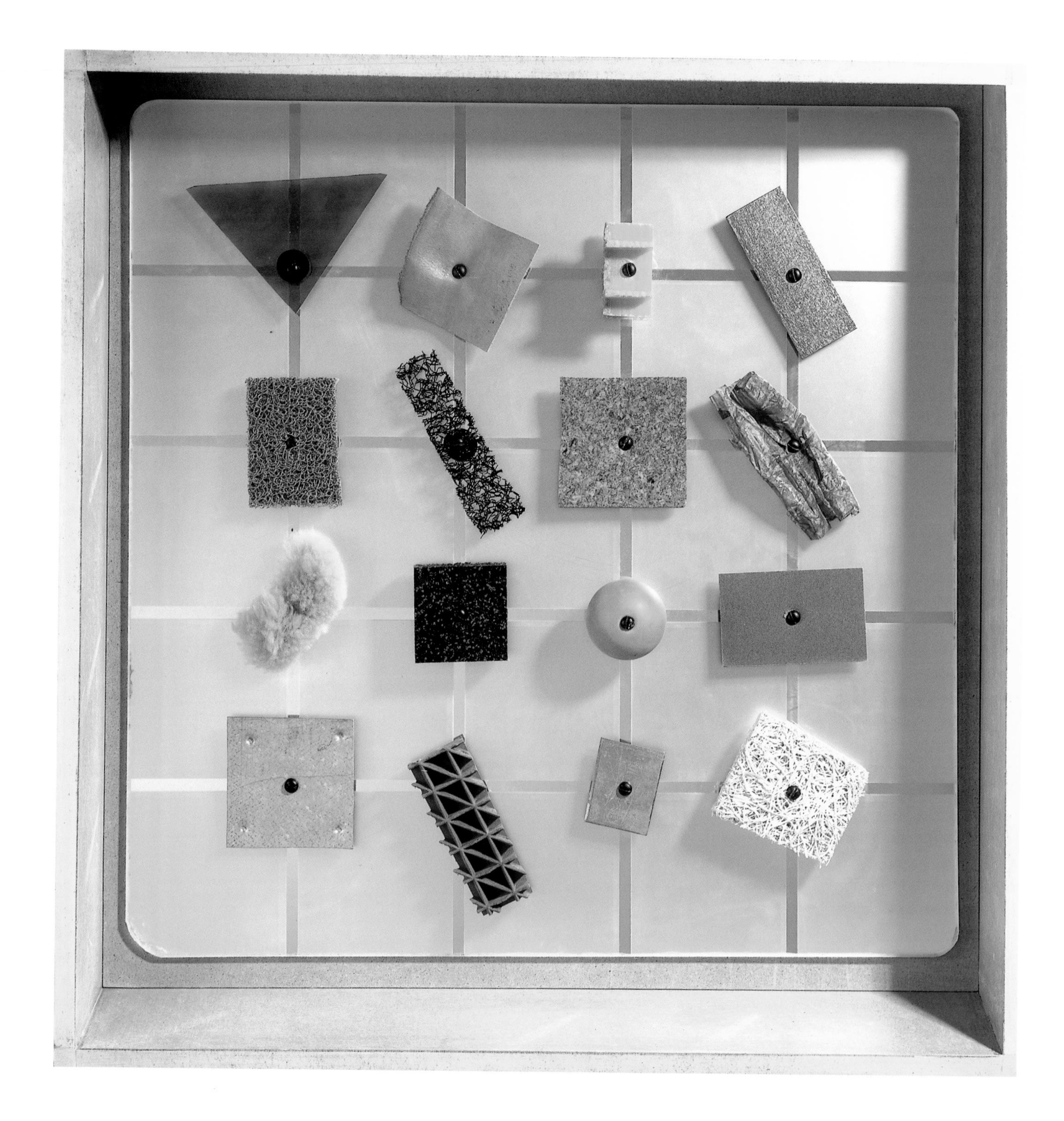

"It is… the role of the designer to educate the public and industry about redefining their perceptions of quality materials. We do not need to abandon all natural materials and methods, but we do need to leave our natural resources in balance by integrating more of the materials that are truly a part of our time."

PHH ENVIRONMENTS

LOS ANGELES

Rinaldo Veseliza

Leather, stone, wool carpet, fabric (natural and synthetic), acrylic solid surface material, natural wood, stainless steel, copper, foam core, plastic tubing, metals

"The board... represents the philosophy of design which is changing so rapidly between the Post-modern and Deconstructionist/Deconstructivist... movements as we head into the New Age where the world is becoming one vast design marketplace. The world is shrinking and our greatest resource is humanity. How we assemble these materials will be determined by our ingenuity."

HAIGH SPACE ARCHITECTS/ DESIGNERS

GREENWICH, CONNECTICUT

Paul Haigh, Barbara H. Haigh

Acid-etched magnesium plate

KING-MIRANDA ASSOCIATI

MILAN

Perry A. King, Santiago Miranda

Etched brass plated with black nickel or silver, turned rosewood, turned Portoro marble, bobbin of cactus fiber

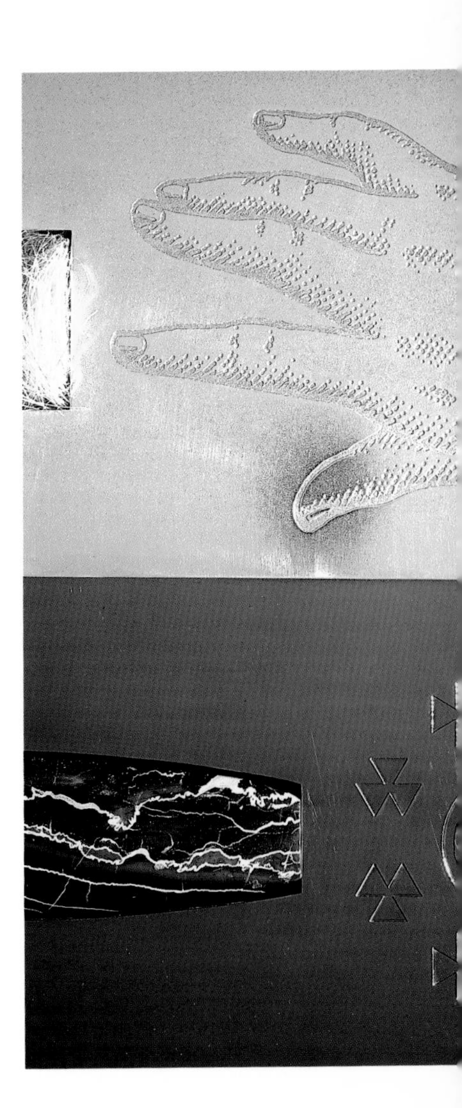

ANDREA BRANZI ARCHITETTO

MILAN

Translucent laminate, woods, marble,

embossed laminate,

reconstituted veneers, liquid crystals

CDM CASTELLI DESIGN MILANO S.R.L.

MILAN

Clino Trini Castelli

Aluminum, reconstituted dyed wood

M. W. STEELE GROUP, INC.

SAN DIEGO

Mark Steele, Jim Gabriel, Juergen Roth, John Downie, Randel Hana, Ken Bierly, Tom Silvers

Copper plate, copper foil, copper rod, rubber sheet, rubber washers, steel bolts, steel pins, concrete

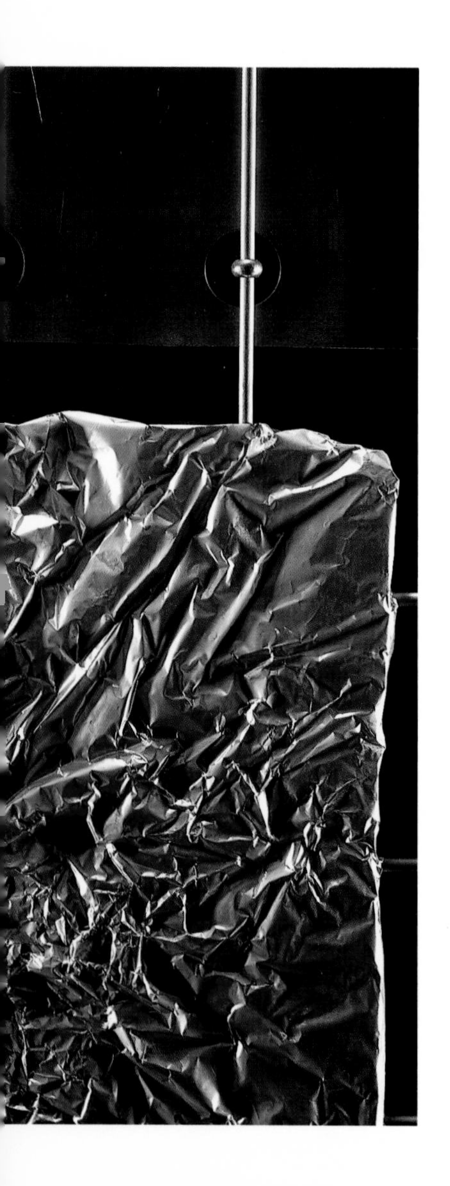

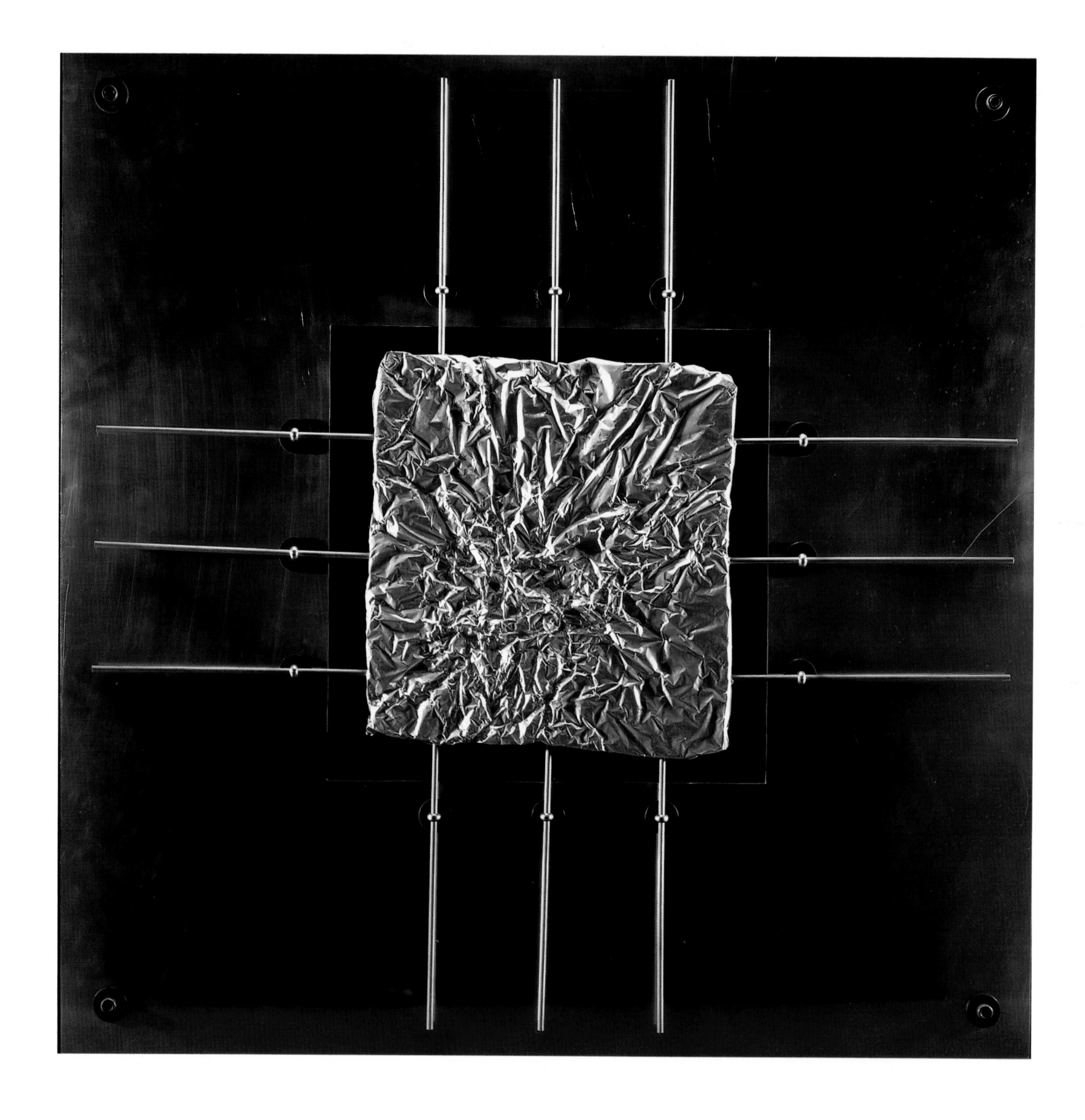

"Copper, a pure and timeless material largely unspoiled by trends, was chosen to express the basic traditional values expected to be the common building-block of future societies."

DANNY LANE

LONDON

Mahogany, oak, mild steel,

Portland stone, glass, wool, gold

NOB + NON

NEW YORK

Earth

A + O STUDIO

SAN FRANCISCO

Aura Oslapas

Particle board, graphite pencils, steel washers, onionskin paper, anodized aluminum layout rulers, plastic scale, metal clip

"It is becoming difficult to focus and delve into our work as more and more information arrives that requires reading, discussion, responses."

DONALD KAUFMAN COLOR

NEW YORK

Donald Kaufman

Multicolored textured coating

CASSON MANN DESIGNERS

LONDON

Dinah Casson, Roger Mann

Plastic hedge, rusty steel sheet,

video monitor

"Plastic, which can be recycled, will be the material of the future.
Here, in its friendliest form, it contrasts with the rusted fragments of the industrial age, which we can no longer support."

ARTORIUM INC.

MONTREAL, QUEBEC

François Dallegret

Polyethylene, resin-interlocking floor tiles

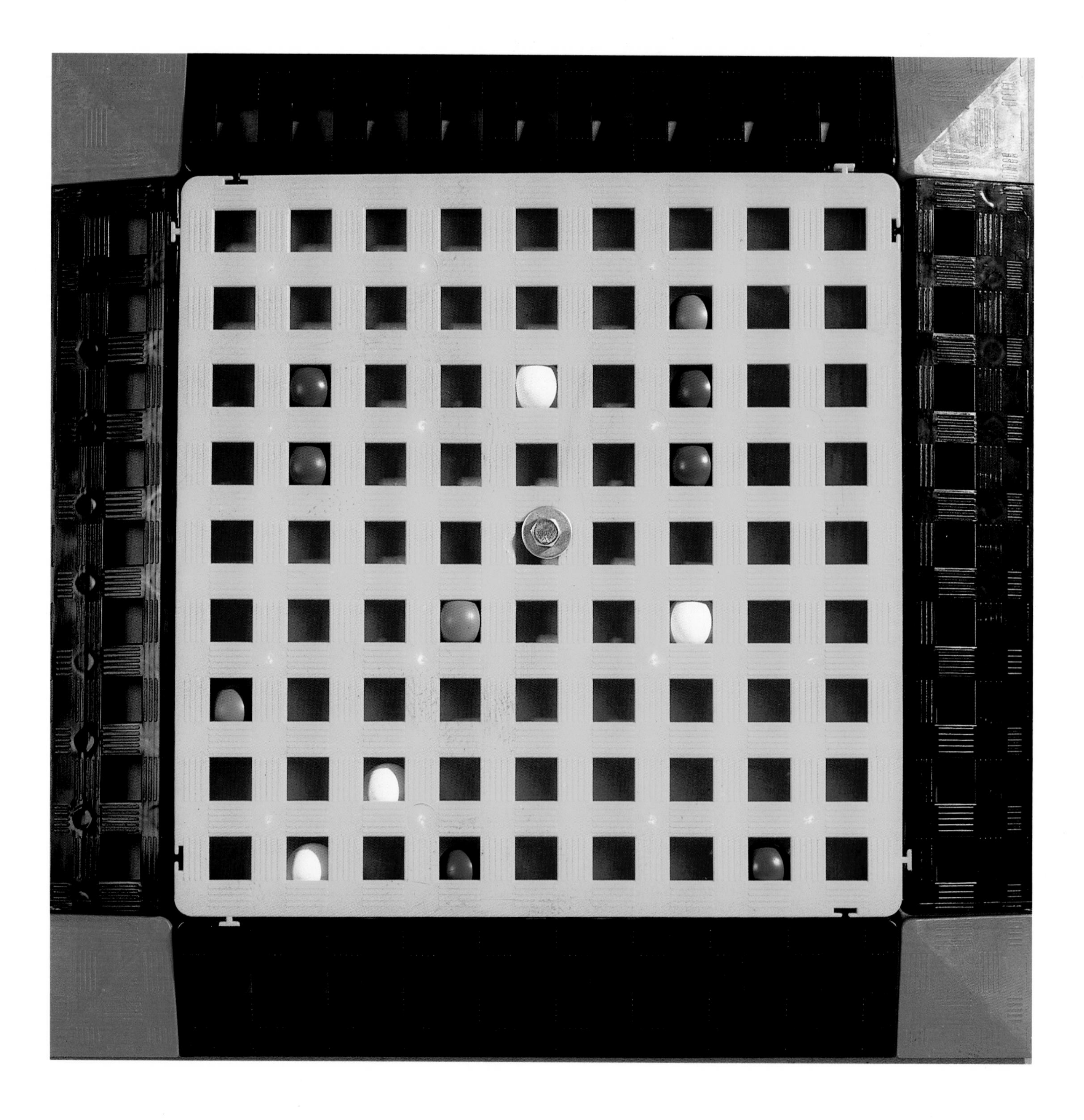

ID TWO

SAN FRANCISCO

Naoto Fukasawa

Concrete board, patterned

laminated plastics

"This plastic is a rare example of a synthetic material because it has some of the random and accidental qualities of natural materials, such as wood or ceramic."

PUI-PUI LI & ERIC JONES

STATEN ISLAND, NEW YORK

Electronic components,

PolyVinylChloride,

anodized aluminum

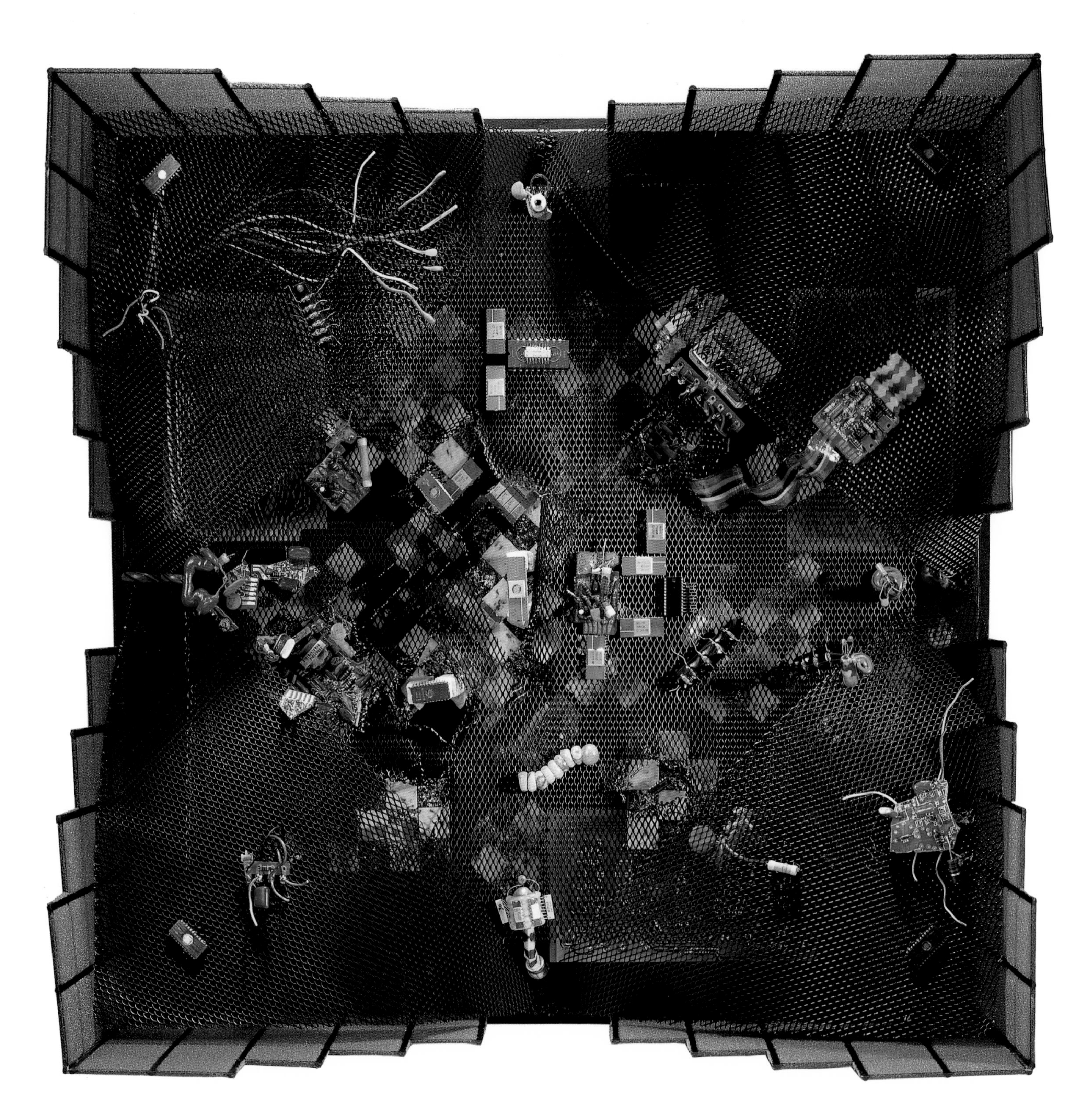

DAN CHELSEA DESIGN

NEW YORK

Dan Chelsea

Epoxy resin, peel ply nylon, phenolic honeycomb with sinusoidal stringers, resined plys of wood and granite, continuous aramid filament yarn and graphite weave cloth

SYNDESIS, INC.

SANTA MONICA, CALIFORNIA

David Hertz, Stacy Fong,

Susan Frank

Pre-cast lightweight concrete,

broken glass, stone,

embossed images, steel,

actual glass, laminated tile,

wood, lead, fiberboard

"It is our intention to explore the honest nature of raw materials and to exhibit the expressive quality of their processes of manufacture and fabrication."

NEDERLANDSE PHILIPS BEDRIJVEN B.V.

EINDHOVEN, THE NETHERLANDS

Robert Blaich, Managing Director,

Oscar E. Peña A., Designer

Aluminum (sand- and water-blasted), wood, polished brass, compact disk, metallic and suede paint

JAMES HONG DESIGN

NEW YORK

James Hong

Broken glass

PEI, COBB, FREED & PARTNERS

NEW YORK

Christa Giesecke

Terrazzo tile

DONOVAN AND GREEN

NEW YORK

Michael Donovan, Nancye L. Green

Dichroic filters

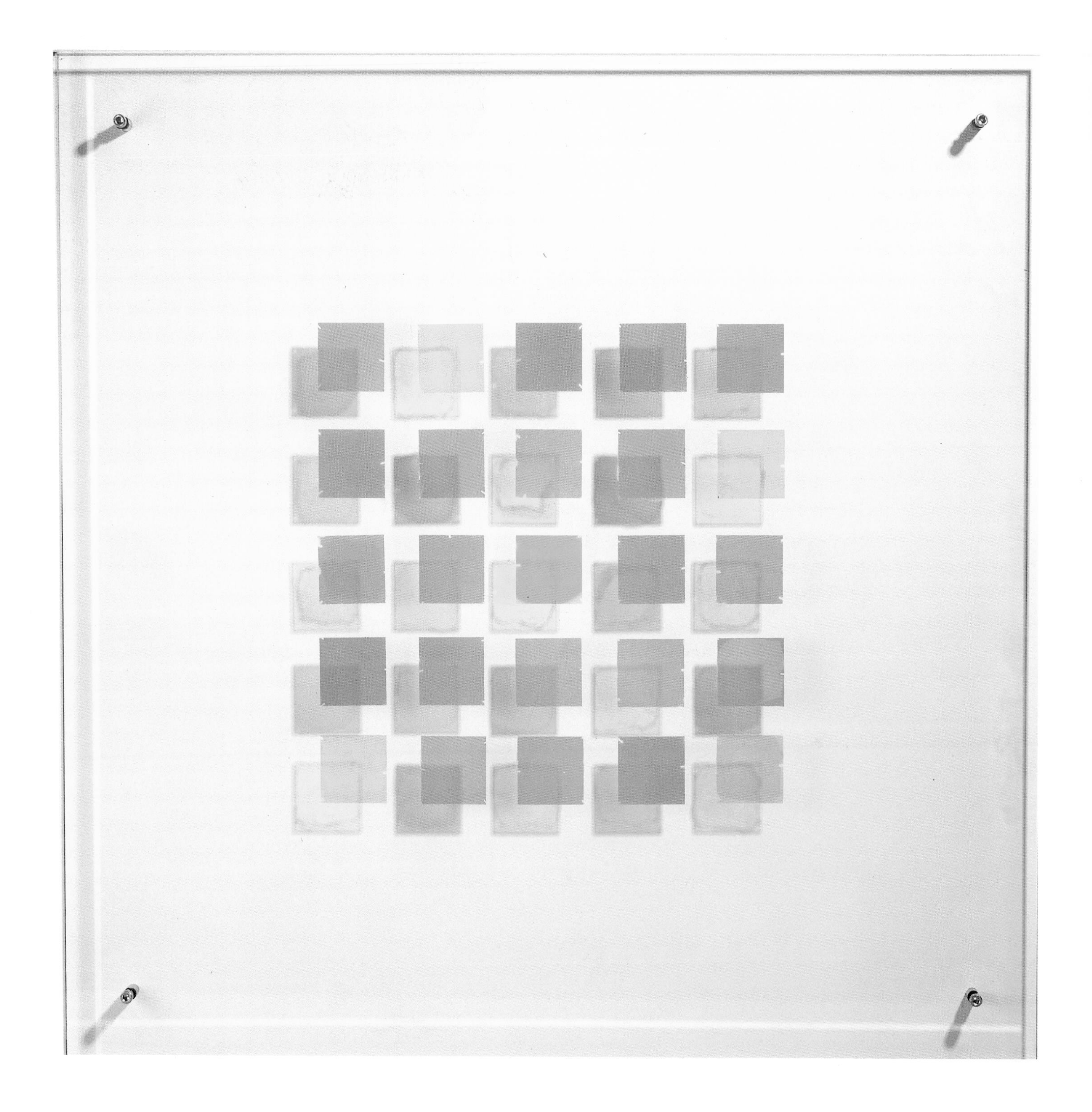

"The dichroic filters are made by applying alternate layers of silicone dioxide and titanium dioxide to a high-temperature glass substrate. . . . The spacing of the layers creates a different index of refraction. . . . As the viewing angle changes, the apparent filter color changes because the angle of refraction is also changing, thereby affecting the portion of the visible light spectrum seen."

KOZO DESIGN STUDIO INC.

TOKYO

Kozo Sato

Water print for plastics, electric luminescence, fluorescent acrylic, photocopy, adhesive for transparency acrylic, white Plexiglas, plastic rod stock, found electronic materials, liquid crystals

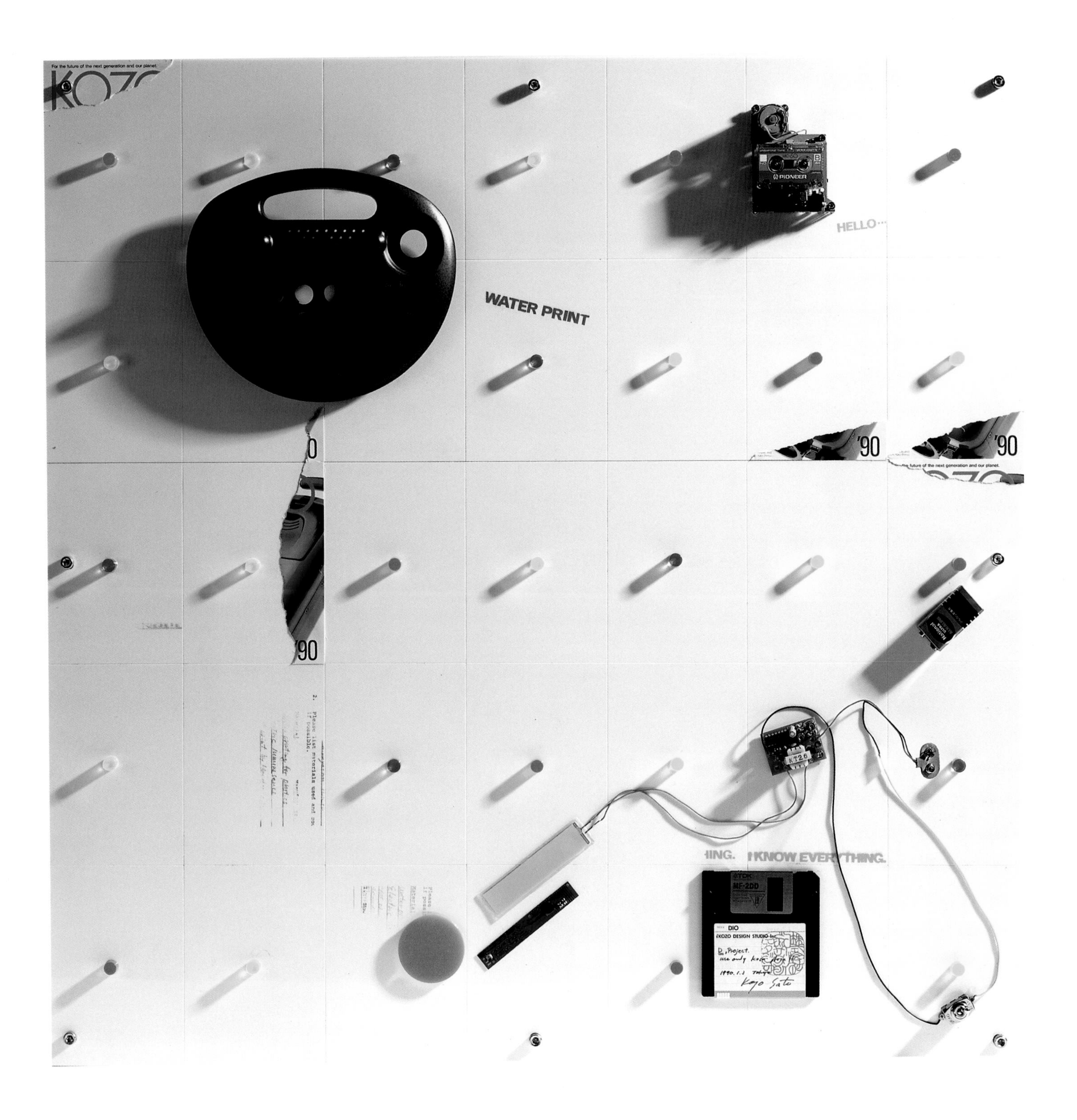

"I hope that we will find a better method to produce highly technological products to suit a pollution-free environment in the next five years."

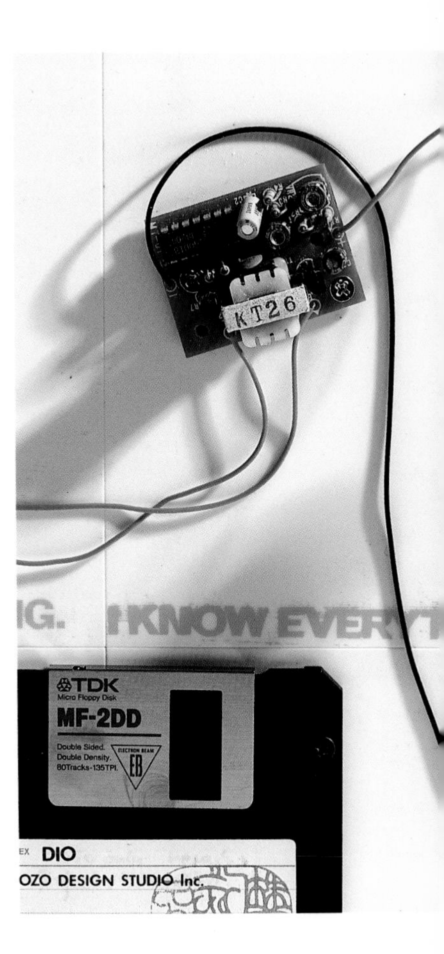

VENT DESIGN ASSOCIATES

CAMPBELL, CALIFORNIA

Stephen Peart

Injection-molded ABS,

knitted nylon fabric laminated to

sheet of neoprene rubber

"These polymer materials represent the vast manipulation that man can have over the performance, shaping, and texturing of objects."

ASSOCIATES & FERREN

WAINSCOTT, NEW YORK

Bran Ferren

Ultrasonic beam proximity detector, glass, laminate, liquid crystal panel, welded aluminum box, electrical controls, fluorescent lights, sponge print on painted cardboard

FTL ASSOCIATES

NEW YORK

Nicholas Goldsmith, AIA

Stretch fabric, neoprene sheeting, plisse ventilation detail in 9032 tedlar polyester, edge clamp/aluminum, woven wire cloth, turnbuckle (brass), brass screen

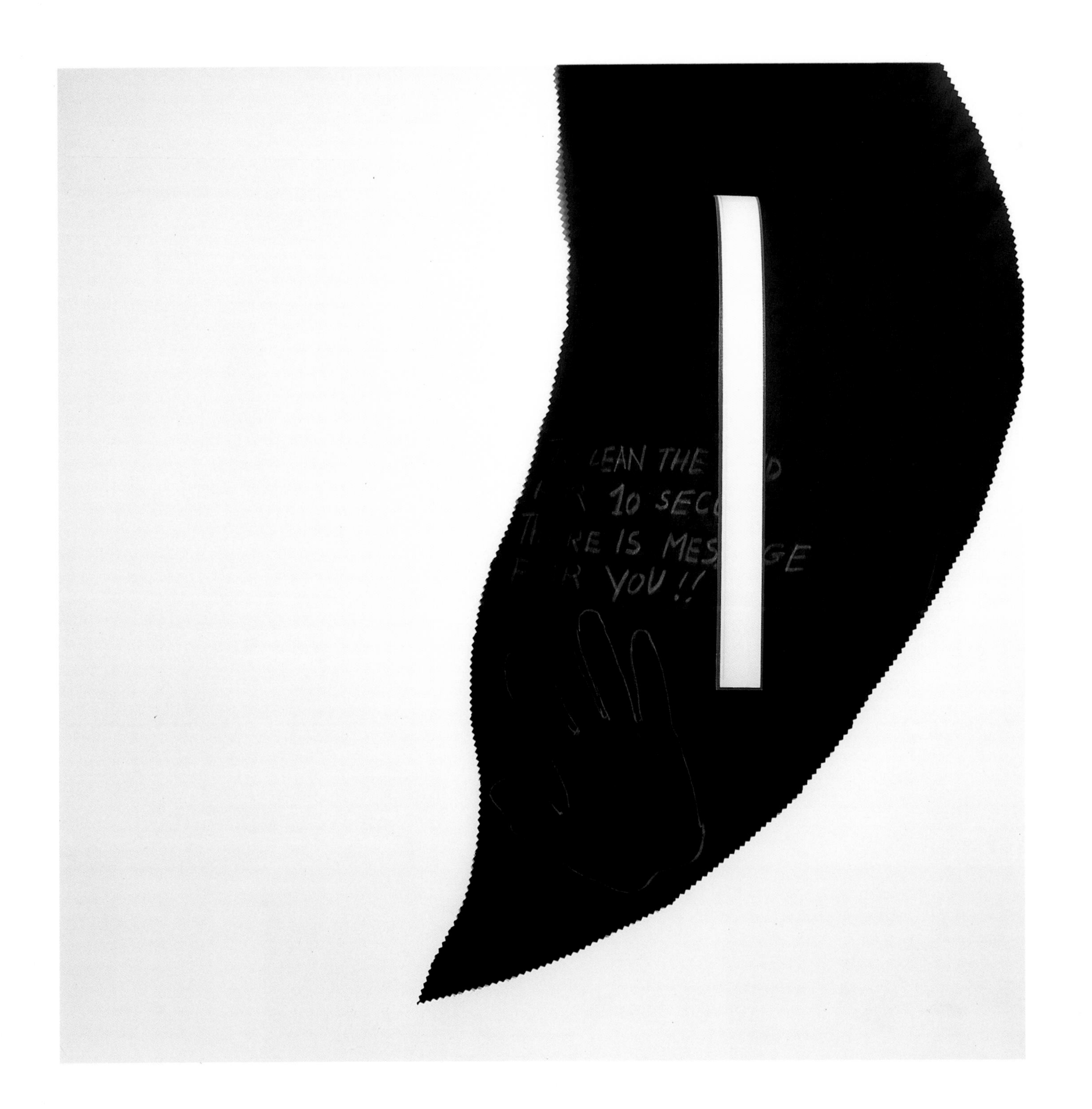

DENIS SANTACHIARA

MILAN

Cardboard, fabric,

electroluminescent

liquid crystal

WILLIAM McDONOUGH ARCHITECTS

NEW YORK

William McDonough

Interference paint,

fresco plaster,

stainless steel grate,

woven stainless steel,

dolomitic limestone,

cherry wood

"We seek out materials that exhibit the character of the craftsperson's hand, such as hand-planed woods and joinery, interference paints, fresco plaster."

ZEBRA DESIGN INC.

NEW YORK

Thomas S. Bley, Steven Holt

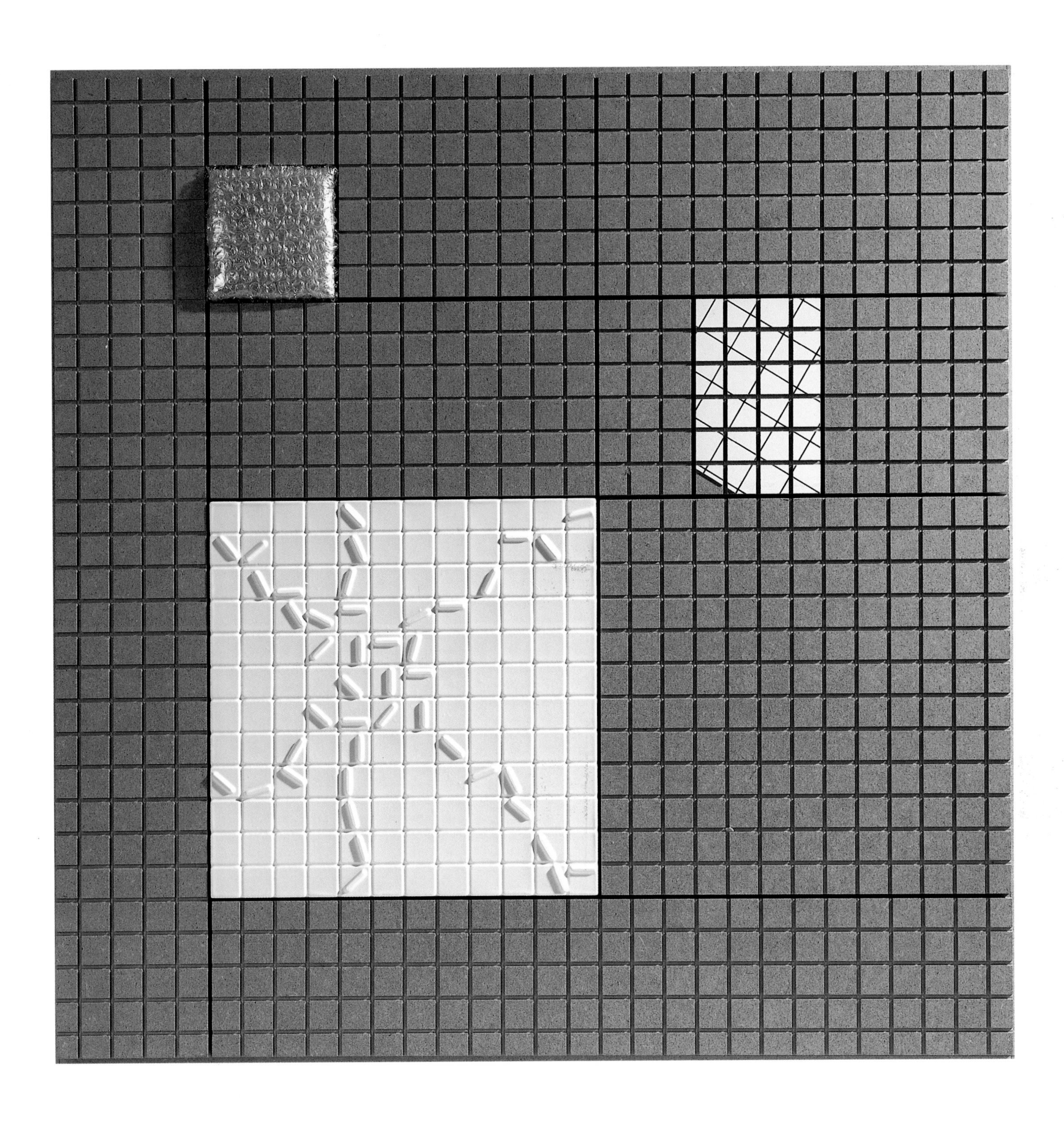

Medium-density fiberboard

vacuum-formed, polysterene,

bubble wrap, laminate

"We like to treat inexpensive things in more precious ways."

SOTTSASS ASSOCIATI

MILAN

Reconstituted veneer

ARQUITECTONICA INTERNATIONAL CORPORATION

CORAL GABLES, FLORIDA

Rug, wallpaper, dichroic glass, anodized metal, wood, molded vinyl tile, tile, concrete tile, steel, marble, found objects

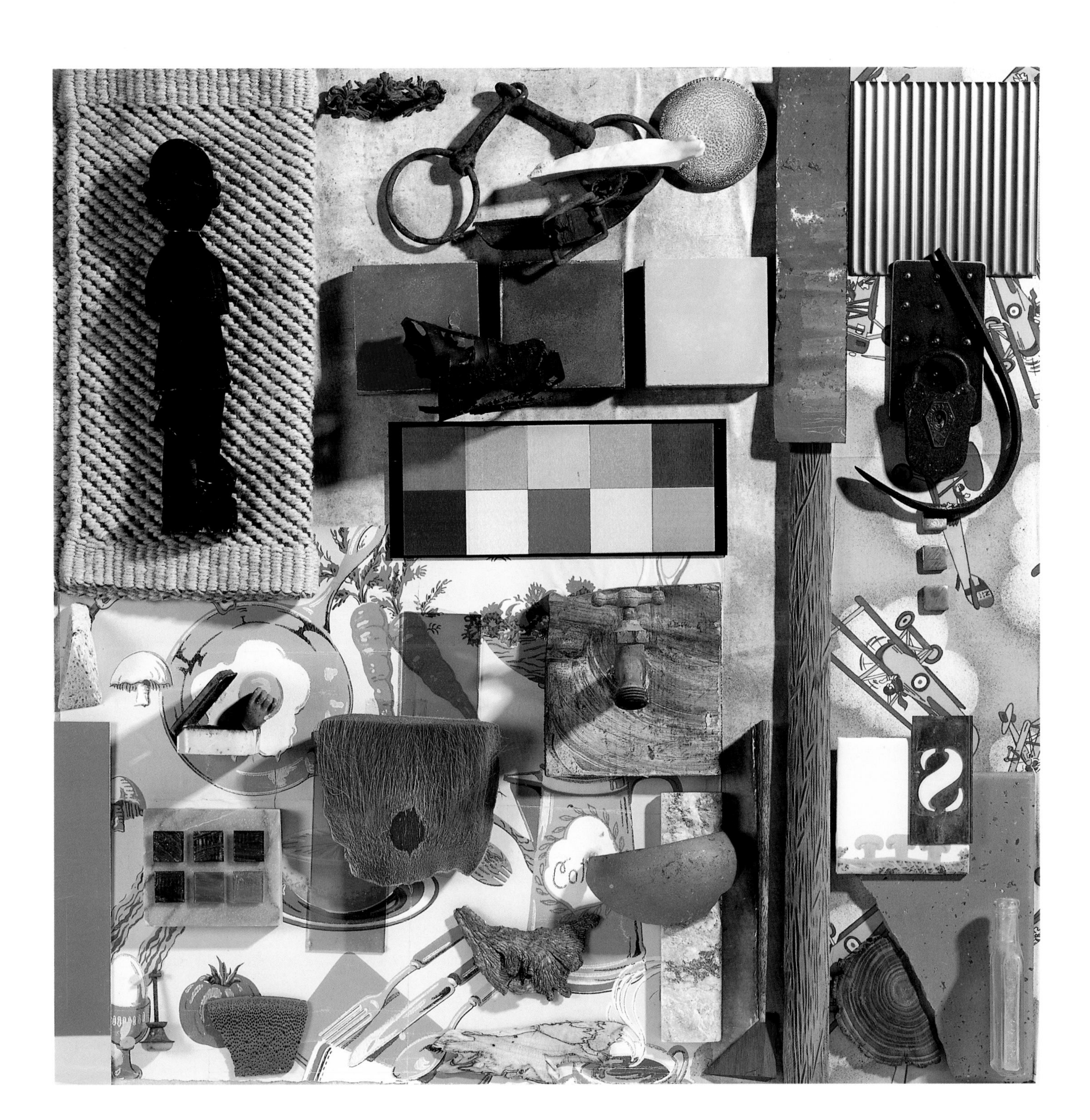

"In the nineties, extravagance feels inappropriate. We want to use straightforward, functional, affordable materials in new ways."

THE WHITNEY GROUP, INC.

HOUSTON

Gary S. Whitney

Glass

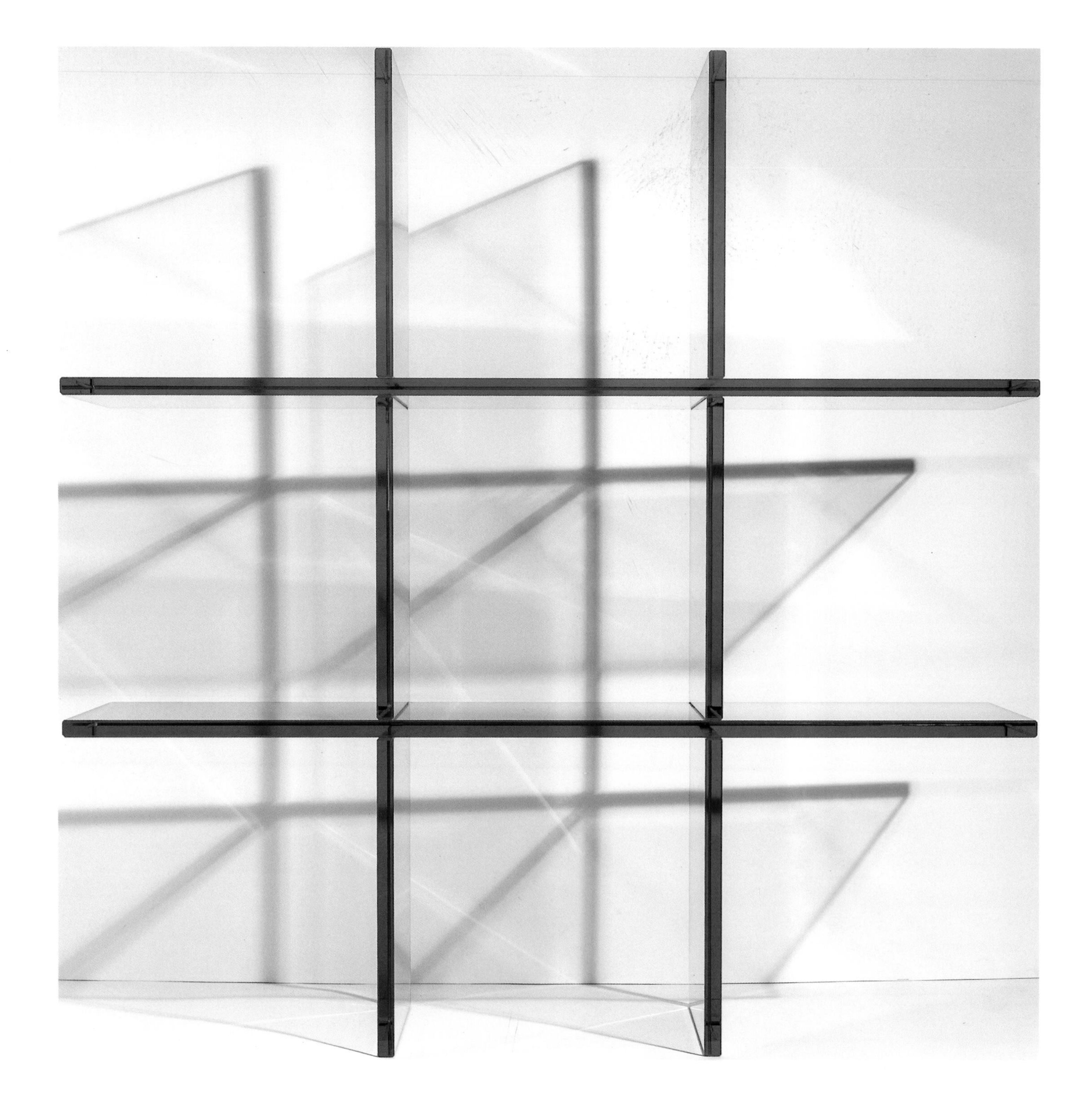

VANDERBYL DESIGN

SAN FRANCISCO

Michael Vanderbyl

Aluminum plate,
aluminum tubing, medite,
cast aluminum, gold leaf,
semi-orange lacquer,
flathead allen screws

JEFFREY BEERS ARCHITECTS

NEW YORK

Jeffrey Beers; Fabrication: Aileron

Bronze, cold-rolled steel, weathered brass, treated steel, laminated rice paper between glass

"The ability to alter, change, and adapt to different conditions and requirements makes metal and glass extremely versatile and attractive materials."

DENNIS OPPENHEIM

NEW YORK

Fabric, objects, silkscreens

RICHARD MEIER & PARTNERS

LOS ANGELES/NEW YORK

Richard Meier

White lacquer in the following finishes: dead flat, flat, satin, satin/semigloss, semigloss, semigloss/gloss, gloss, high gloss, high gloss — buffed

"White is in fact the color which intensifies the perception of all the other hues that exist in natural light and in nature.... Yet when white is alone, it is never just white, but almost always some color that is itself being transformed by light and by everything changing in the sky, the clouds, the sun, the moon."

ORLANDO DIAZ-AZCUY DESIGNS

SAN FRANCISCO

Orlando Diaz-Azcuy

Standard brass-plated linoleum nails, white paint, medium-density fiberboard

"Because of the availability of finishing materials on the market, it is rare that designers concern or direct their attention to creating new ones. Most of the materials are here; it all depends how one uses them."

ROGERS AND GOFFIGON LTD.

GREENWICH, CONNECTICUT

James F. Gould, John J. Flynn, Jr.

Plexiglas boxes, cotton,

linen, woven fabrics of wool,

silk, leather

THUN DESIGN

MILAN

Matteo Thun

Pyramid acrylic on mirror glass,
gold glass — mosaic,
perforated metal on aluminum,
millepunti glass,
optical glass on mirror,
Waxos marble,
Oece lacquer on glass

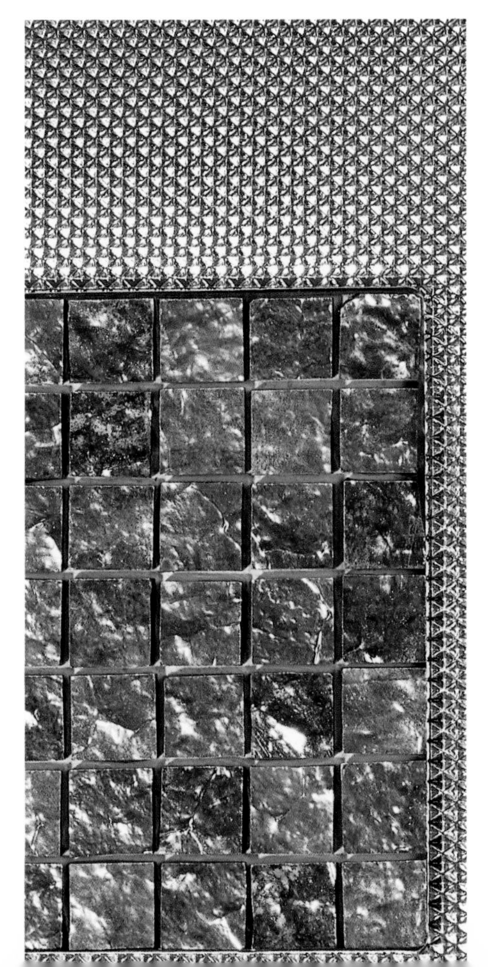

"The idea is to use high-tech materials that have a natural look."

RICARDO BOFILL TALLER DE ARQUITECTURA

PARIS

Annabelle d'Huart

Vinyls, fabric, wood veneer,

machined stone, printed tile

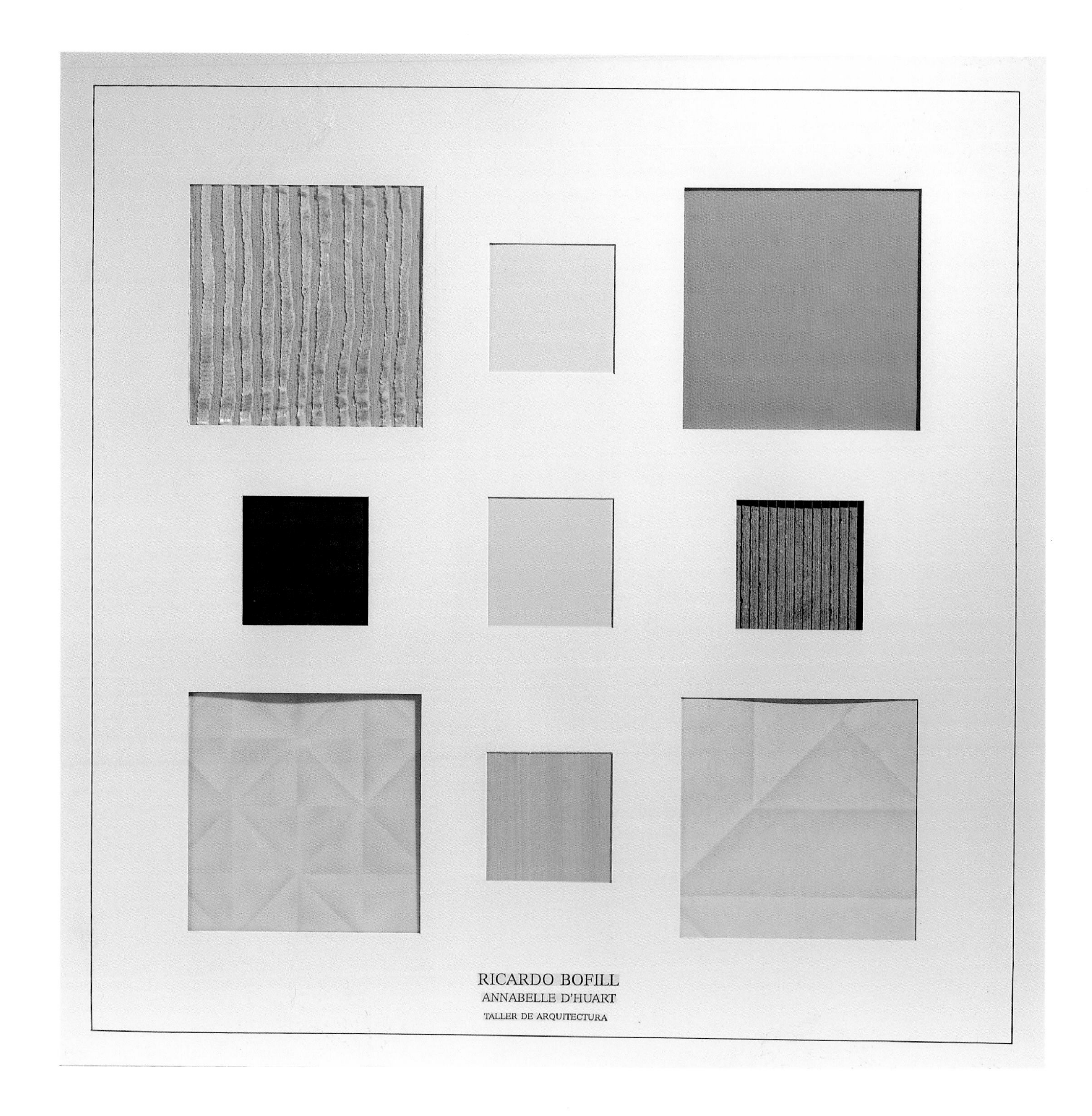

"These materials describe an ethereal aesthetic, one which strives to clarify space, not cover it. The aesthetic of the nineties will concern sensitivity; our hope is to employ materials that will enhance this interior state."

HERBERT PFEIFER

SAN JOSE, CALIFORNIA

Carpet, ceiling tile,

wood, fiber

ceramic aggregate

MARTINE BEDIN

MILAN

Gold-leaf tile/glass,

wood solids,

slate, marble

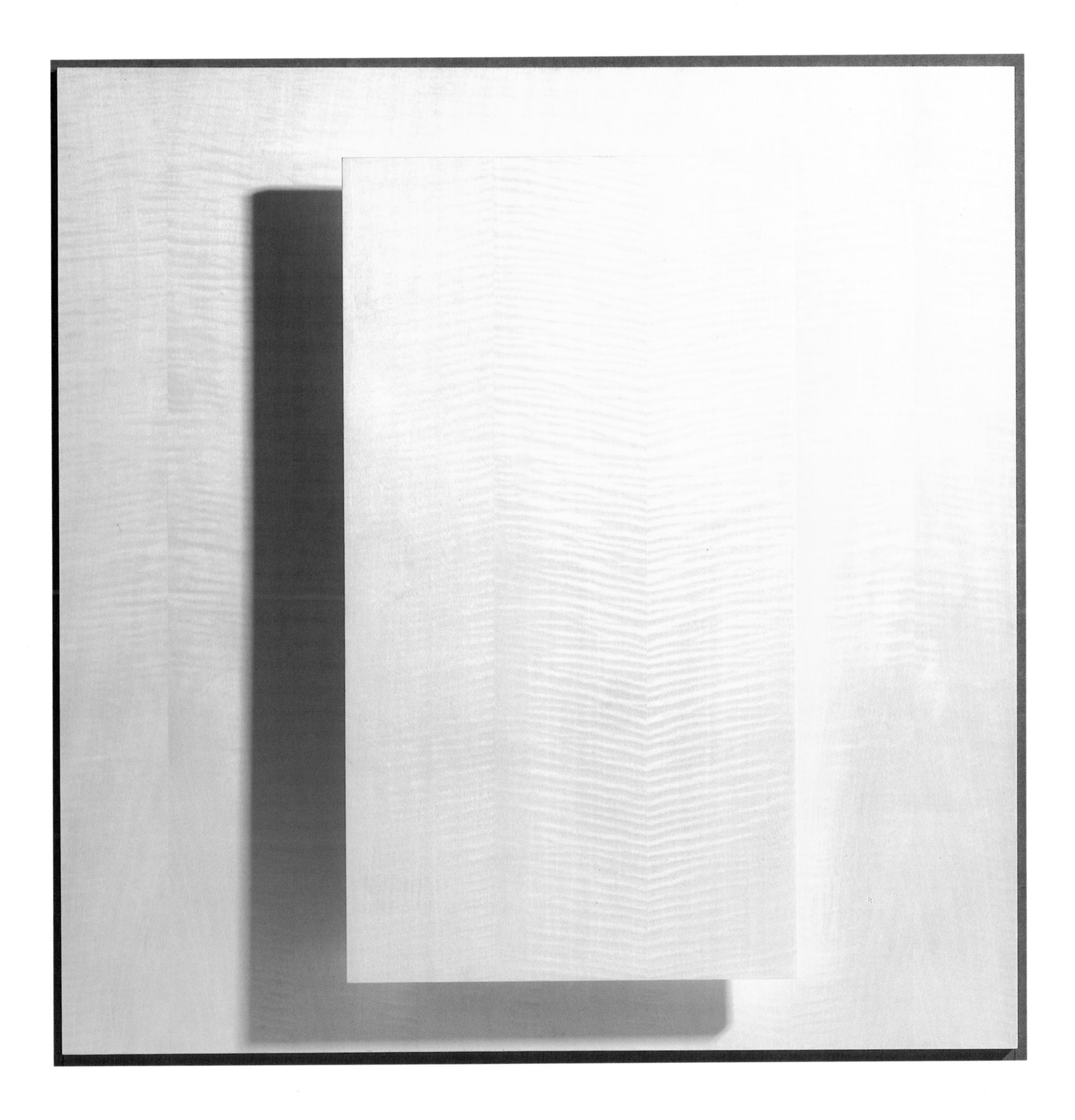

PETER STATHIS/ SCOTT ZUKOWSKI

NEW YORK/INDIANAPOLIS

Dyed natural fiddleback anigre,

fluorescent pigment

TORCK-NOIROT

PARIS

Emmanuelle Noirot,

Emmanuelle Torck

Felt, wool crêpe, copper nails, brushed glass, rice papers, wood solids, sandblasted anodized aluminum, printed fabrics

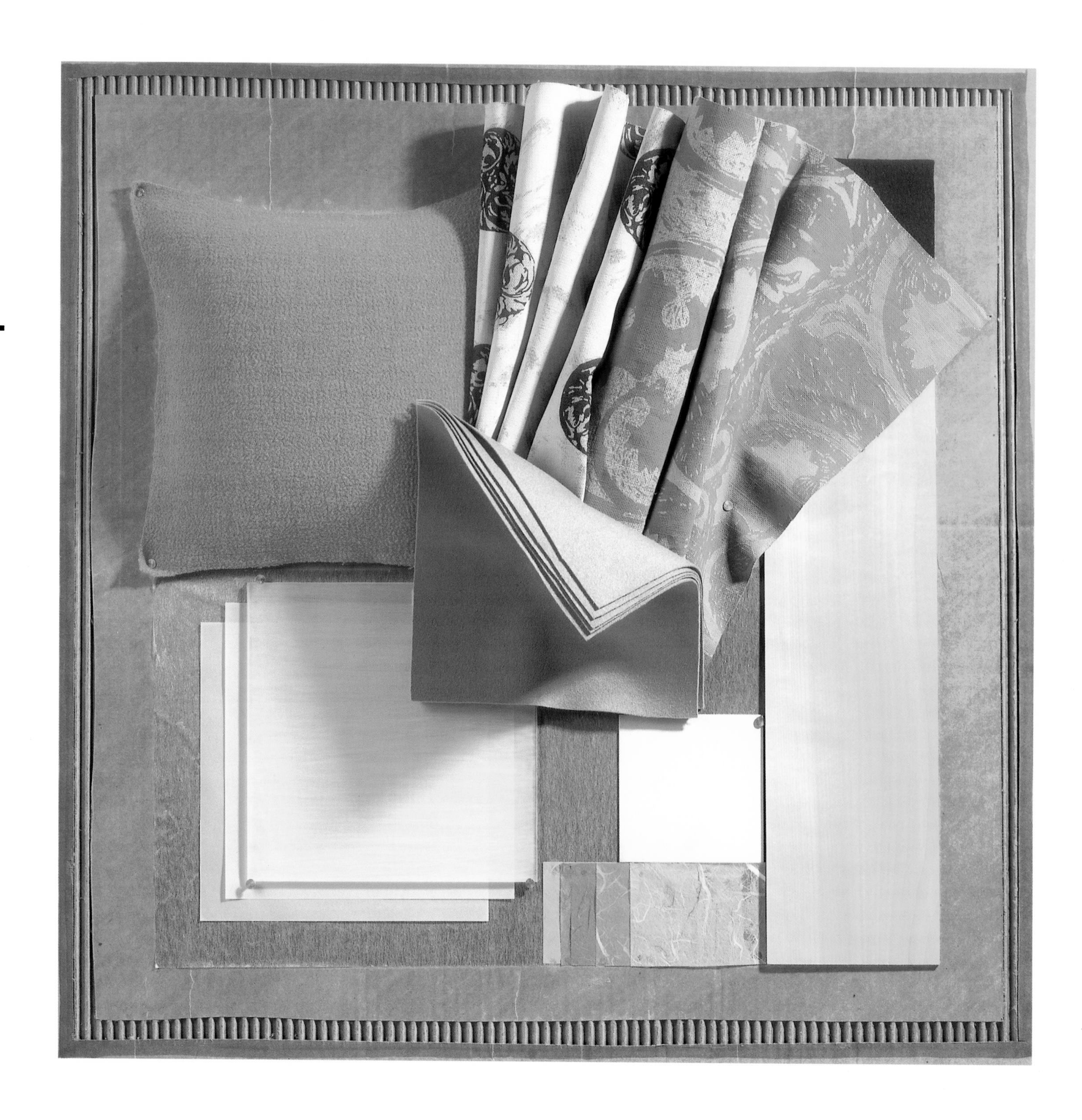

"We prefer to emphasize the tactile sensation often left out of modern design."

ERIC OWEN MOSS—ARCHITECT

CULVER CITY, CALIFORNIA

Eric Owen Moss, Scott Nakao, Dana Swinsky; Fabricators: Tom Farrage, Scott Gates

Aluminum angles, bent re-bar, threaded rod, oriented strand-board, purple heart wood

DESIGN STUDIO TAD

TOKYO

Tadao Shimizu

Assorted rice papers,

gold leaf,

metal leaf

"Materials are a way of linking the past and future, in the same way that individuals do. What is important in this bonding is preserving and expressing the past while simultaneously expressing hope and dreams for the future."

ORDIEG ASOCIADOS

BARCELONA

Gabriel Ordieg Cole

Stone, corrugated aluminum sheet, silkscreened glass, perforated board

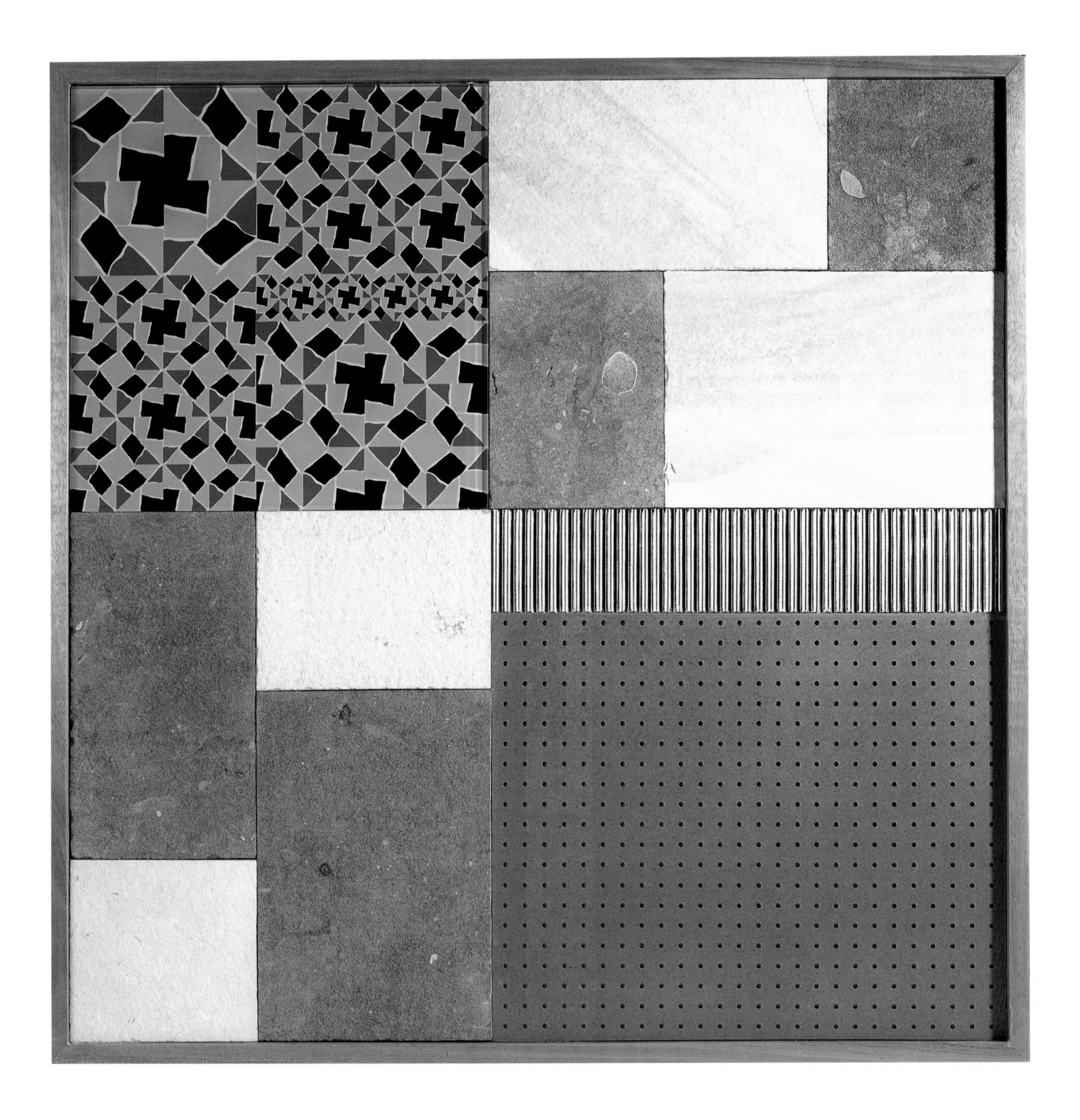

"...In the next few years the mixture of materials (traditional and high-tech, organic and nonorganic) will be common in interior design... I also think there is a difficult but necessary balance between materials which must be sought in order to avoid banality."

LARSON ASSOCIATES

CHICAGO

George Larson, Susan Larson,

Jennifer Denlinger

Glue chip glass,

aniline-dyed

bird's-eye maple,

woven leather,

etched metal finishes,

corrugated fiberglass,

handwoven bauxite

"...texture and surface will be to the 1990s what color and form were to the 1960s.... Also, there will be a demand for materials to look rich, yet cost little."

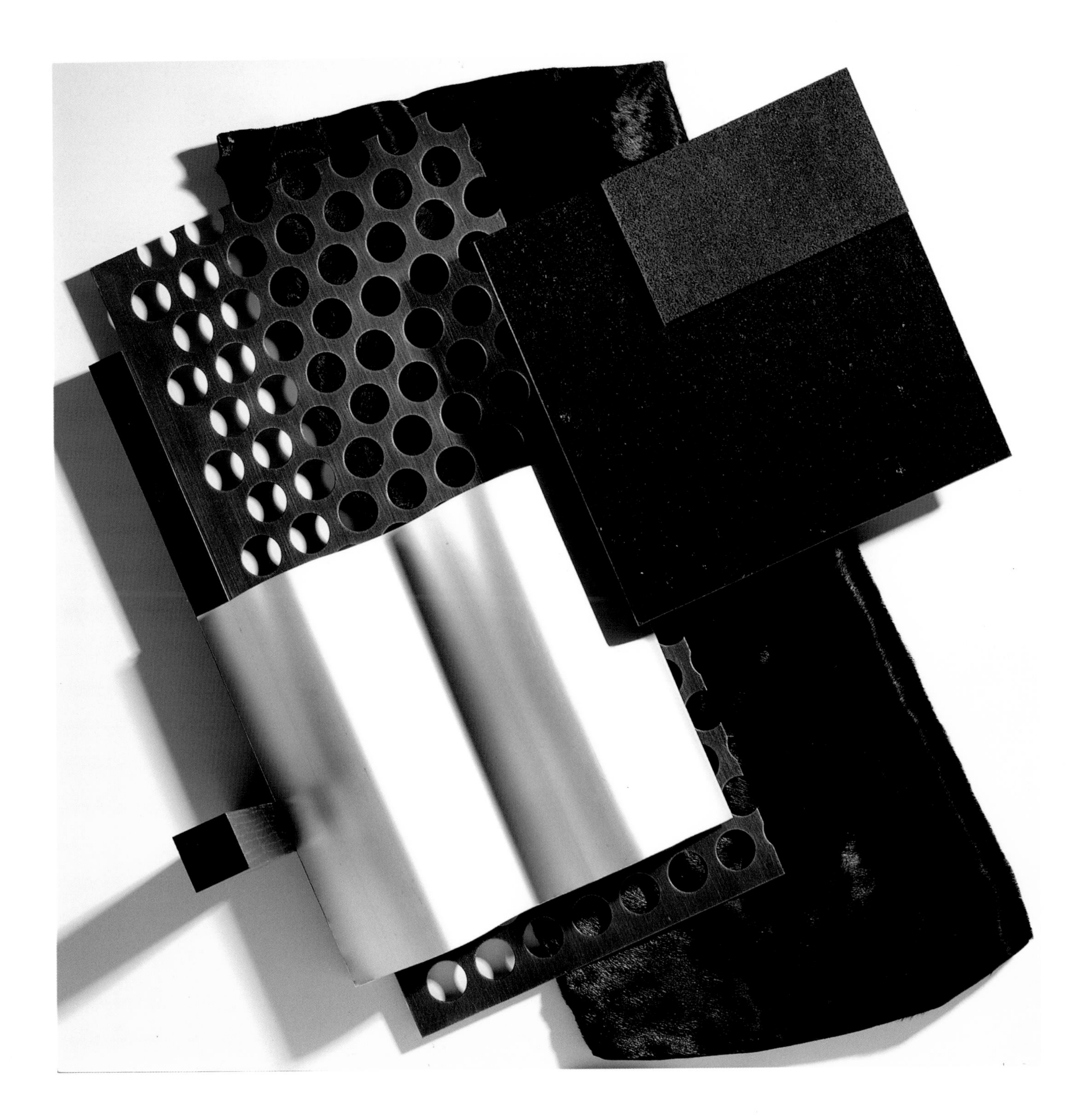

TRIX AND ROBERT HAUSSMANN ALLGEMEINE ENTWURFSANSTALT

ZURICH

Trix and Robert Haussmann

Granite, rubber floor,

perforated sheet iron

(zinc finish), black foal skin,

stained oak, beech wood,

anodized corrugated aluminum

KOHN PEDERSEN FOX CONWAY ASSOCIATES, INC.

NEW YORK

Patricia Conway

Mica, granite, treated metals, woven metals, woven leather, velvets, lace, cherry wood, embossed fabrics, stone, shell aggregate, found objects, silver dollar plant leaves, laminated metallic plastics

STUDIO 80

TOKYO

Ikuyo Mitsuhashi

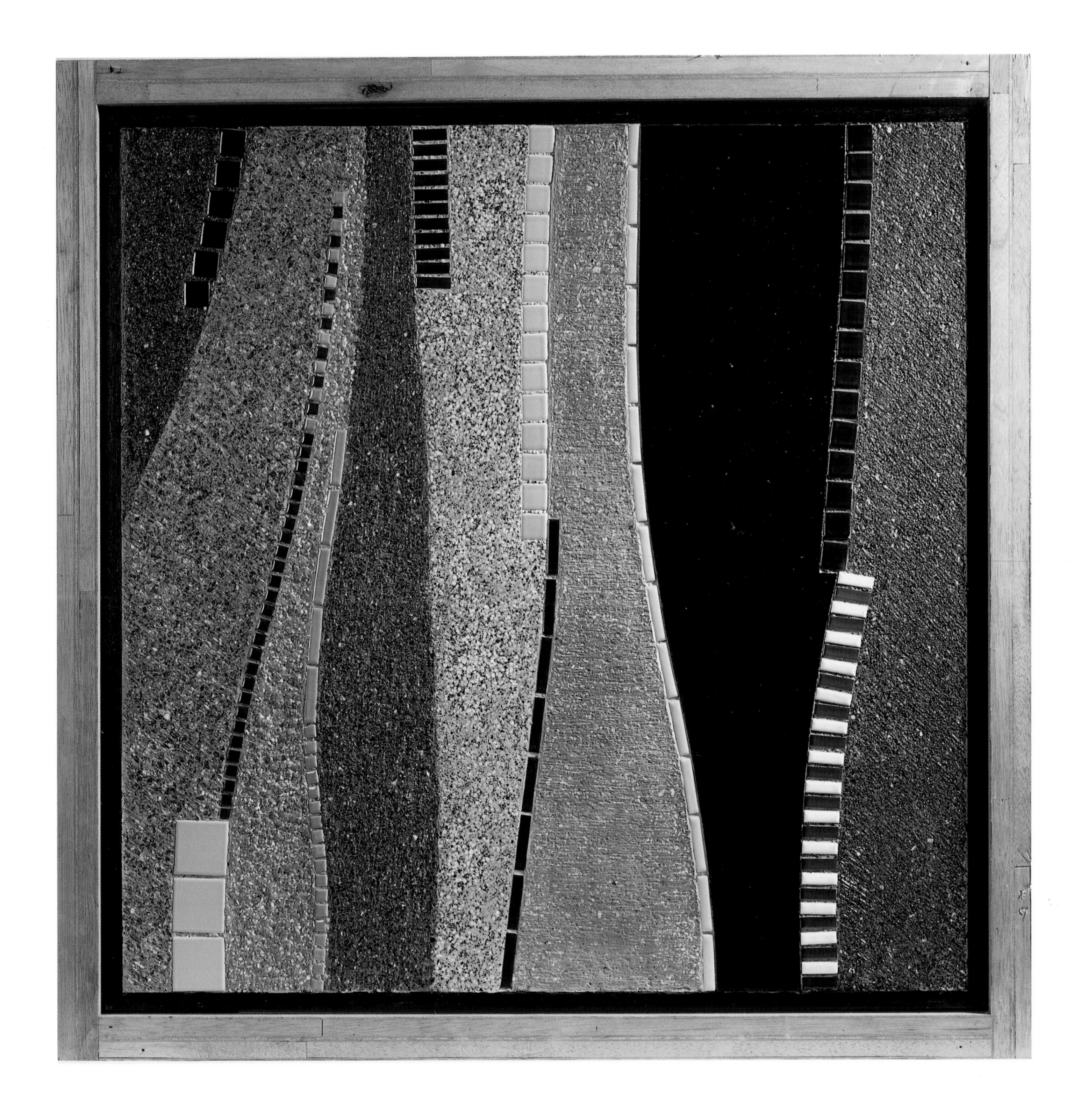

Black granite,
colored concrete
with pebbles

ECART SA

PARIS

Andrée Putman

Steel mesh, synthetic horsehair fabric, wood, metallic gold-leaf backed glass, etched metal

DEPOLO/DUNBAR INC.

NEW YORK

Lydia dePolo, Jack Dunbar, Steven Brooks, Elyse Hommel-Cohen

Silk, silk/linen, ceramic tile,

etched pewter,

dyed reconstituted wood,

flame-finished granite,

etched stainless steel,

ribbon, silk cord

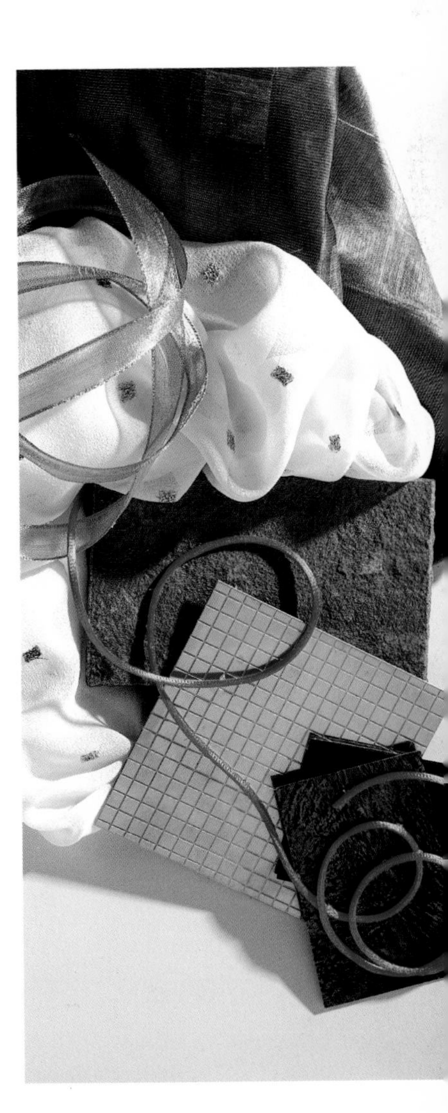

*"**We** expect to use both natural and manufactured materials with an emphasis on the latter. In addressing this prospect, we foresee greater manipulation of surface, having unexpected textures and colors inspired by a vast repertoire of chemical dyes and manufacturing processes."*

PETER MARINO & ASSOCIATE ARCHITECTS

NEW YORK

Peter Marino

Black Belgian marble, limestone, mahogany, goatskin, lacquered wood, grass-cloth wall covering

VICENTE WOLF ASSOCIATES, INC.

NEW YORK

Vicente Wolf

Bronzed Plexiglas, perforated metal, leather, suede, wood solids, fabrics, plastic ivy, copper

"When warm, elegant, luxurious, and functional elements are combined they create a comfortable and inviting environment."

ADAM D. TIHANY INTERNATIONAL LTD.

NEW YORK

Adam D. Tihany, Paulin Paris

Sandblasted glass,

mirror,

stainless steel

"In the center of the panel, the reflection of the only material that can make the difference: you."

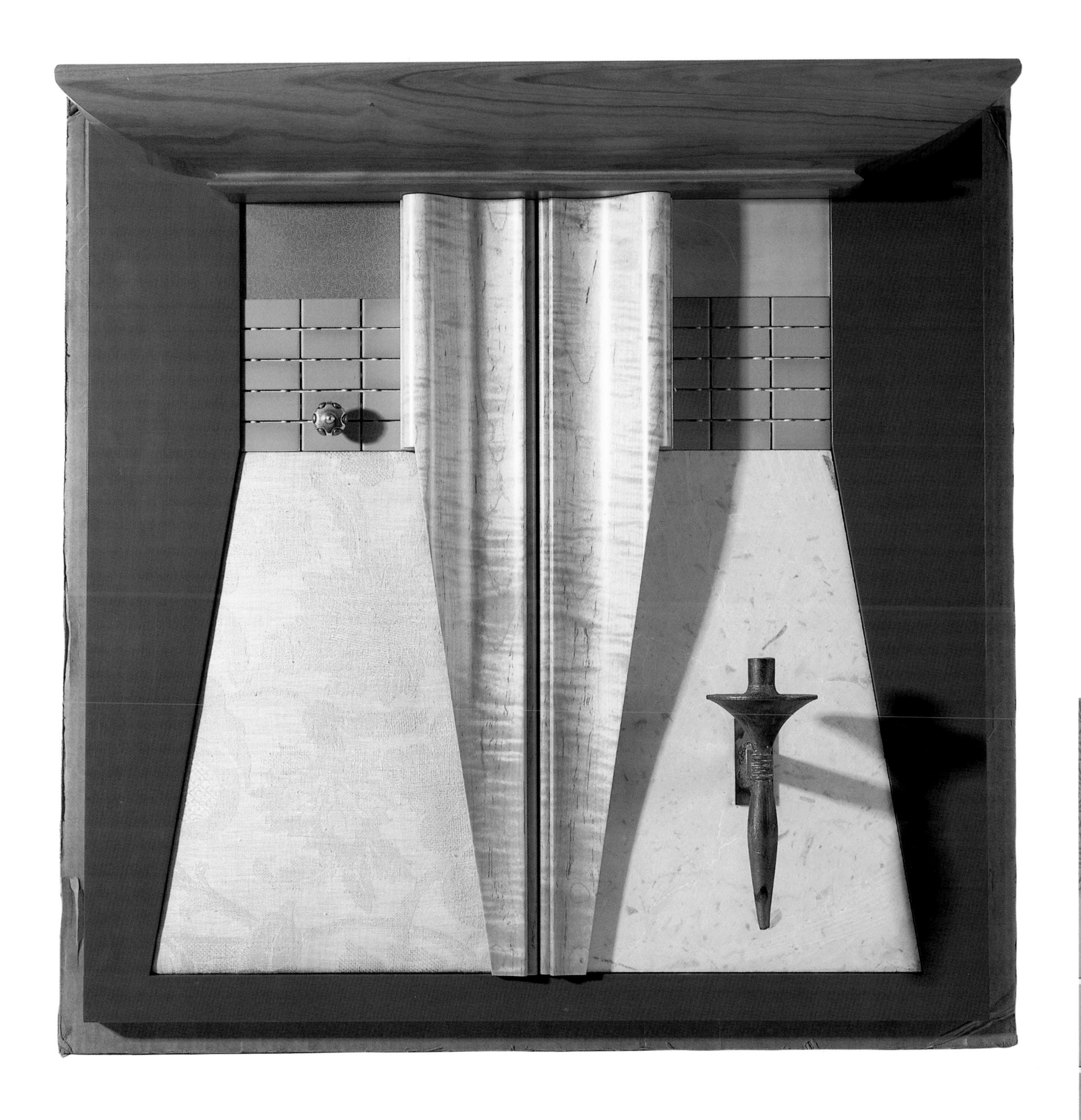

BENTLEY LAROSA SALASKY, ARCHITECTS AND DECORATORS

NEW YORK

Ronald Bentley, Salvatore LaRosa, Franklin Salasky

Plastic laminate, ceramic tile, wallpaper, fabric, silver, brass, cherry wood, tiger maple, leather

LEMBO BOHN DESIGN ASSOCIATES, INC.

NEW YORK

Laura Bohn, Joseph Lembo

Wallpaper, rough-cut cedar, rusted metal rod, silk velvet, natural linen fabric, aluminum screen

"We see a trend toward materials that evoke tranquility and have a strong connection to nature."

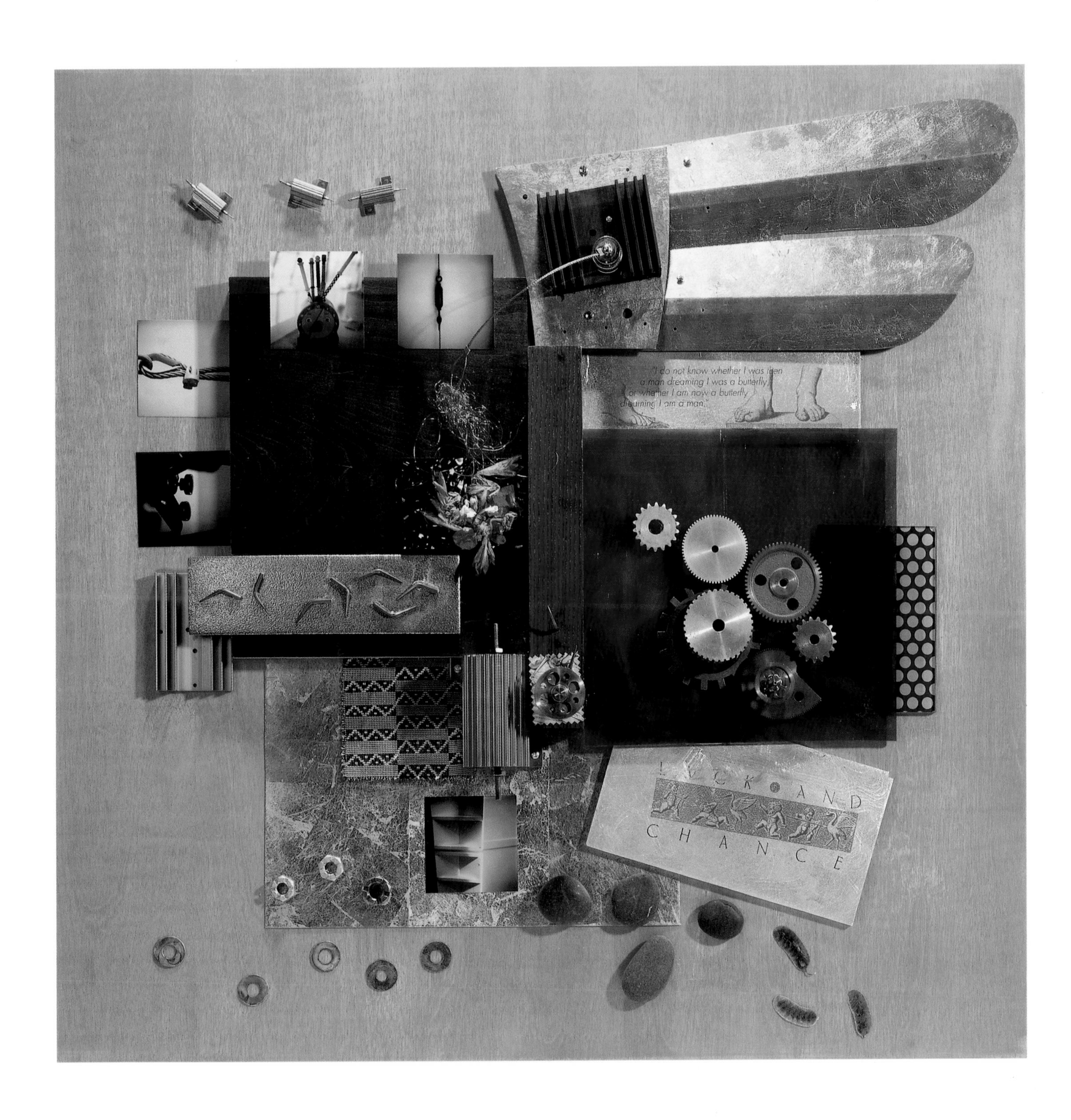

SUSSMAN/PREJZA & CO.

CULVER CITY, CALIFORNIA

Lance Glover, Chuck Milhaupt

Iridescent glass, frit glass,
gold, silver, copper leaf,
found metal objects, copper, brass,
anodized aluminum, marble,
terrazzo marble

"A thoughtful attitude toward materialism is called for, one which values the treasures that surround us and moves us to utilize our resources rather than to squander them."

JUXTAPOSITION OF MATERIALS

HARRY TEAGUE ARCHITECTS

ASPEN, COLORADO

Suzannah Reid, Glenn Rappaport, Harry Teague

Metallic coating over oriented strandboard, rusted corrugated steel, glass backed with galvanized metal, rubber washers with steel bolts

ROSENBERG KOLB ARCHITECTS

NEW YORK

Eric J. Rosenberg, Michele Kolb,

Nina Wong;

Fabrication: Gordian Raake

Arizona flagstone, absolute green marble, iridescent glass, crackle glass, carbon fiber, copper cloth, natural birch bark, Baltic birch veneer

"Our work seeks to rethink the use of familiar materials, to use new materials in innovative ways. Our presentation is about contrasts: rough vs. smooth, dark vs. light, primitive vs. high tech...."

JOHNSON FAIN AND PEREIRA ASSOCIATES

LOS ANGELES

R. Scott Johnson

Architectural metals, glass, tile, cardinal pink graphite, lunar pearl granite, Verde Issoire marble, Rose Corail limestone, Sunflower limestone, miniblinds, wood veneer, vinyl flooring, leather, sisal, wall covering, lightweight concrete, plastic flooring

"Our collage defines a dialectic about the future of building materials. . . . While the membrane grids and their materials will be accessible to increasingly specialized groups, the proliferation of cheap, adaptive, and largely man-made materials will indulge the varieties of more broadly educated members in an increasingly mobile, informed society."

FUMIO SHIMIZU ARCHITECTS

TOKYO

Fumio Shimizu

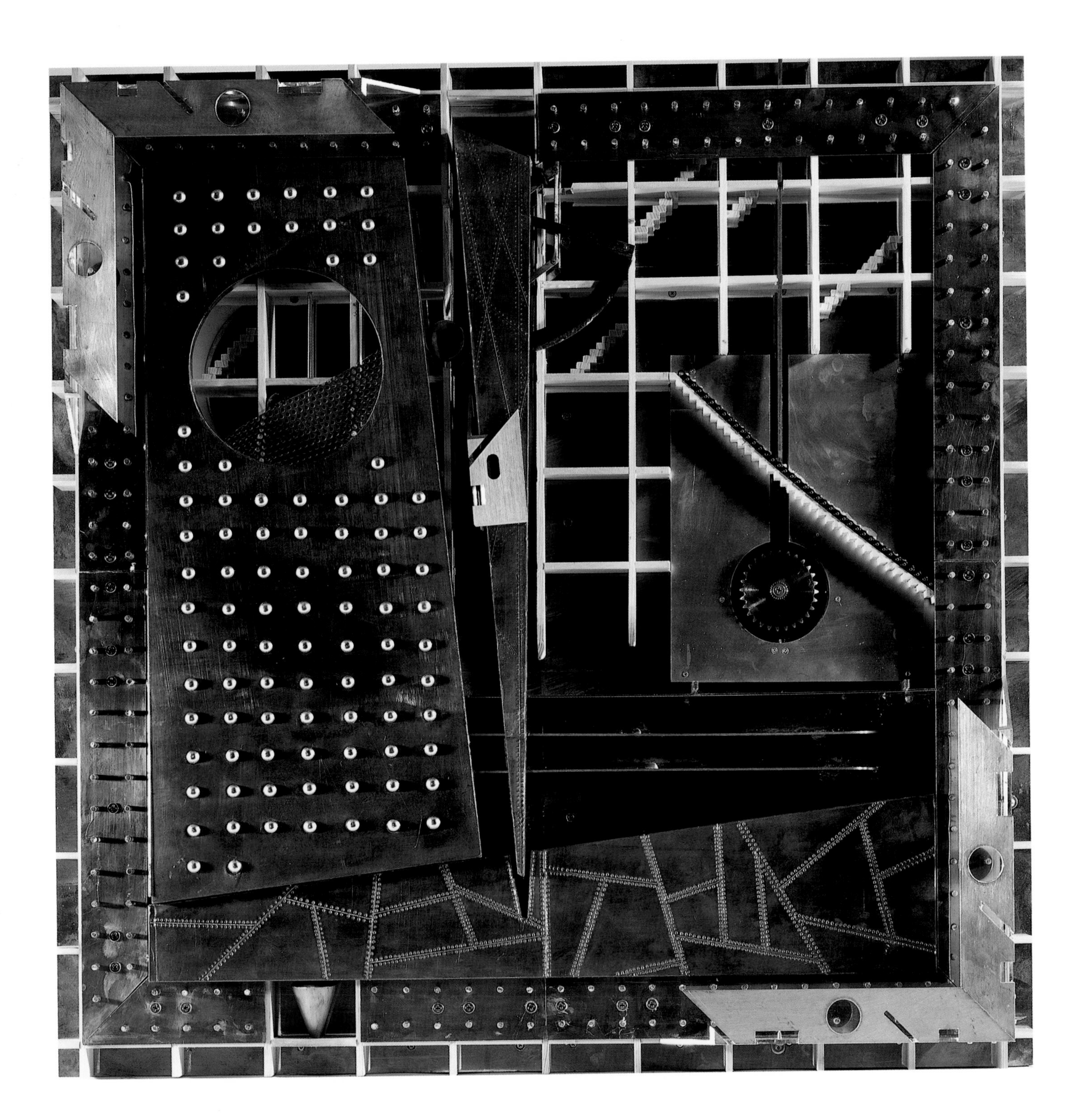

Wood, aluminum, lead, iron,

fragrant wood shavings,

chemically treated brass

EVANSON STUDIOS

NEW YORK

James Evanson

Steel, copper,

low-voltage (12v) light,

halogen light (20w),

wood, lacquer, graphite

GODLEY-SCHWAN

BROOKLYN, NEW YORK

Lyn Godley, Lloyd Schwan

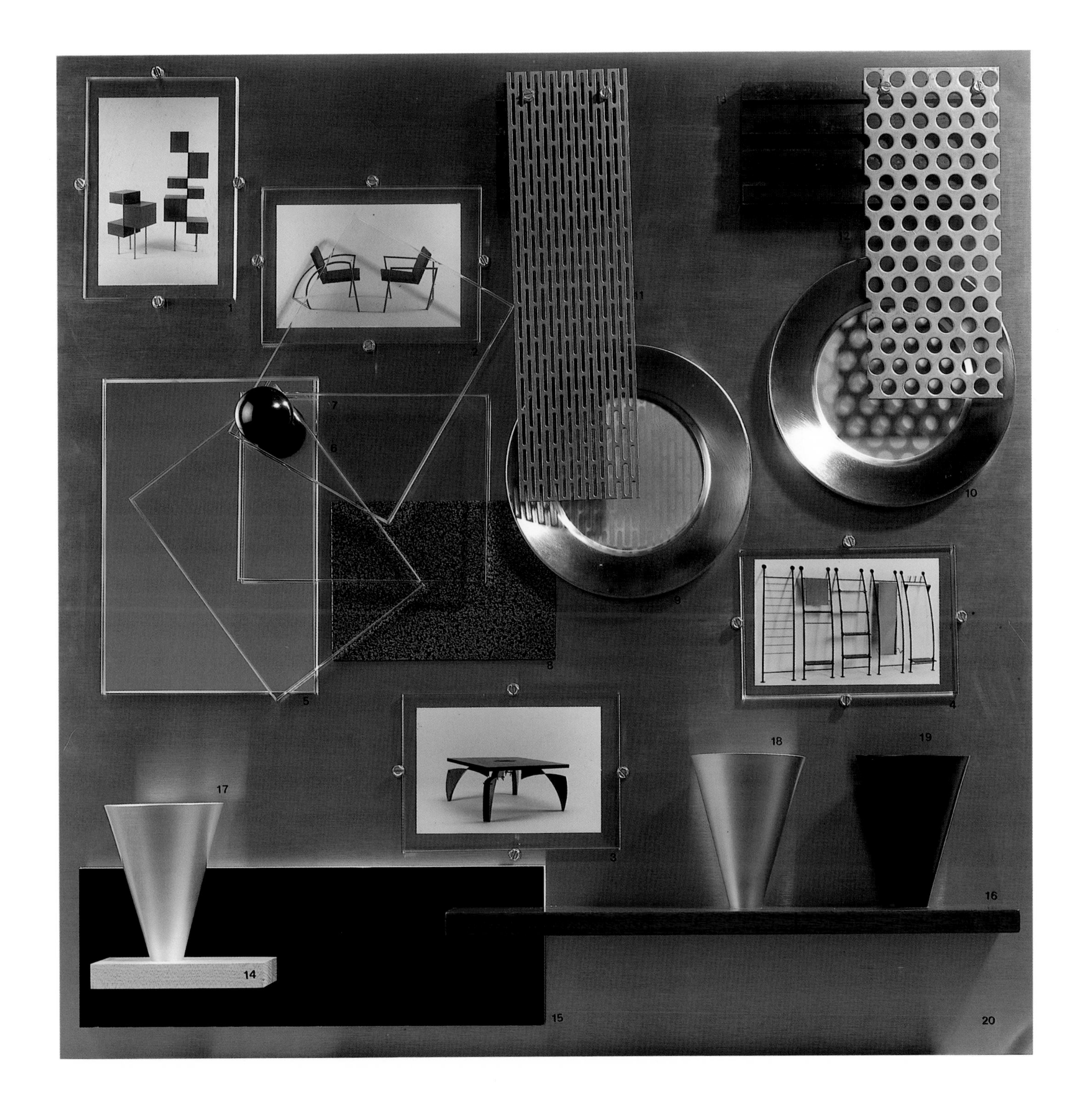

Glass, mirror,
stainless steel,
perforated steel,
extruded rubber,
wood (walnut, oak,
mahogany),
anodized aluminum,
black acrylic,
silver-vein
powder coatings

"We feel an honesty emerging about the use of materials, employing the inherent qualities of natural materials and a mixture of soft and hard materials to create a more balanced feeling than apparent in the 1980s."

VIGNELLI ASSOCIATES

NEW YORK

Lella and Massimo Vignelli,

David Law

Sheet lead, gold leaf,
sandblasted glass,
particle board with
special white finish,
random-brushed
aluminum plate,
copper sheet with patina,
sandblasted cold-rolled steel,
hot-rolled steel with
special black finish,
hot-dipped galvanized steel

*"All materials reflect or absorb light according to their surface finish. Light is the master of form....
We sense the importance of a viewer's perception and of articulate materials to achieve deliberate connotations, since whatever is perceived is retained and analyzed one way or another."*

DESIGN PARTNERSHIP

SAN FRANCISCO

Andrew Belschner, Joseph Vincent

Oriented strandboard,

plastic laminate, leather,

galvanized metal

KALLMANN McKINNELL & WOOD ARCHITECTS, INC.

BOSTON

Michael McKinnell

Slate, ceramic tile mosaics, drapery, standing seam copper, carpeting, glass tile, marble, limestone, face brick, mahogany, photography, coated metals, metal laminates

LEE H. SKOLNICK ARCHITECTURE + DESIGN

NEW YORK

Lee H. Skolnick, John Kashiwabara

Particle board, homasote,
rubber mat, plastic laminate,
metal mesh screens,
rubber-coated wood dowel,
cork, rubber tube, acrylic sheet,
sandpaper, copper sheet,
vinyl flooring

"In the international cultural polyglot that characterizes the close of our century, the individualized regional languages of figurative decoration and ornamentation will give way to the more universal, evocative, and sensual language of compositions of natural and industrial-made materials."

ECCO

NEW YORK

Eric Chan

Perforated metal,

urethane rubber,

synthetic granite,

wood, metal rods

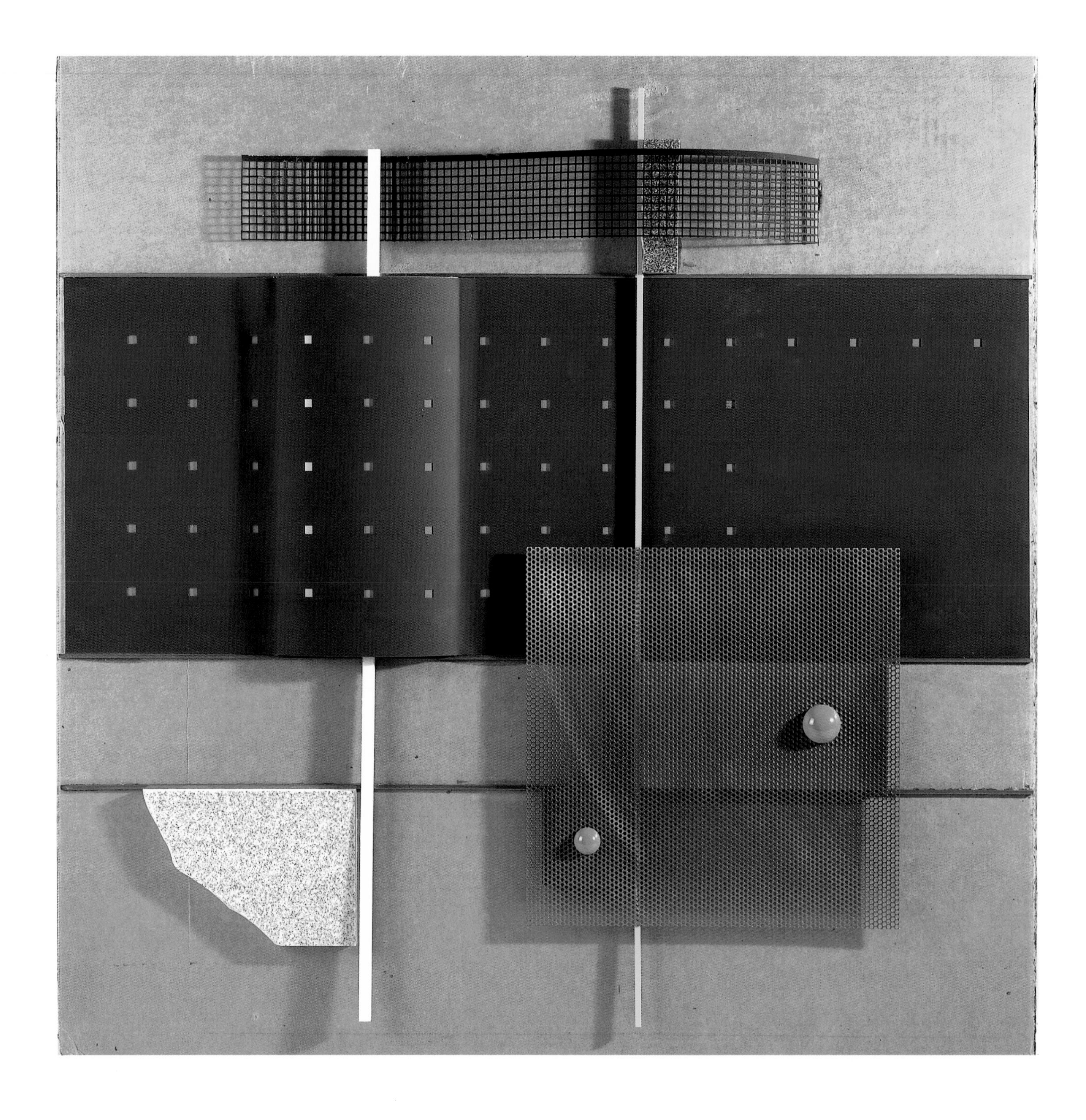

NANDA VIGO

MILAN

Seashells embedded into white aggregate, polished and unpolished aggregate, broken glass laminated to aggregate

BRIGGS MacDONALD

NEW YORK

Fluted glass, chipped glass, fiberglass, black and white plaster, metal leaf, terrazzo, ingrained flooring, embossed metal. Granite, linoleum, woven steel, metallic fabric, acrylic, scratched stainless, burlap-patterned glass, stainless mesh, gilded mesh

"I see a disillusionment with synthetic materials and a finer honing of contrasts when different materials are employed together."

DRAKE & BOUCHER

NEW YORK

Robin Drake

Panel fabric, structural fabric, stair tread, granite finish, rubber floor tile, slatwall, wire grid, natural maplewood flooring, anodized aluminum, faux-etched glass, handwoven cotton

FREDERICK FISHER ARCHITECT

SANTA MONICA, CALIFORNIA

Frederick Fisher

Terrazzo, desert sunset and red slate, stainless steel, ceramic mosaic, brass mesh, cocabola, ebony wood, glass, clear and obscure wire, fabric (2), Texas shell limestone, glass mosaic, hot-rolled steel, aluminum, plastic tortoiseshell, particle board, lead, plastic mats, embossed metals, fiber-coated papers, rice paper

"Material duality is the primary notion behind the selection of these materials."

THE MODERNS

NEW YORK

Jon Otis, Janine James

Perforated steel, reconstituted bird's-eye veneer, etched glass, slate, steel wire, hardware

"The next industrial revolution requires the devising of soft and conceptual qualities that are more sophisticated and complex."

BOYM DESIGN STUDIO

NEW YORK

Constantin Boym

Plastic laminate, carpet, pine, gold leaf, reconstituted wood, wall covering

ANDERSON/ SCHWARTZ ARCHITECTS

NEW YORK

Frederic Schwartz, assisted by Joanne Robinson

Wood studs, sheetrock, copper piping, hot-rolled steel, marble, silk

*"***Z***ora is a collage of conventional and nonconventional materials that are juxtaposed to establish a dialogue between the practical and the poetic."*

JOHN LONCZAK DESIGN

NEW YORK

John Lonczak

Mirror

*"**N**ever before has the time been more ripe for the appropriate use of material."*

ROBERT W. EBENDORF

SANTA MONICA, CALIFORNIA

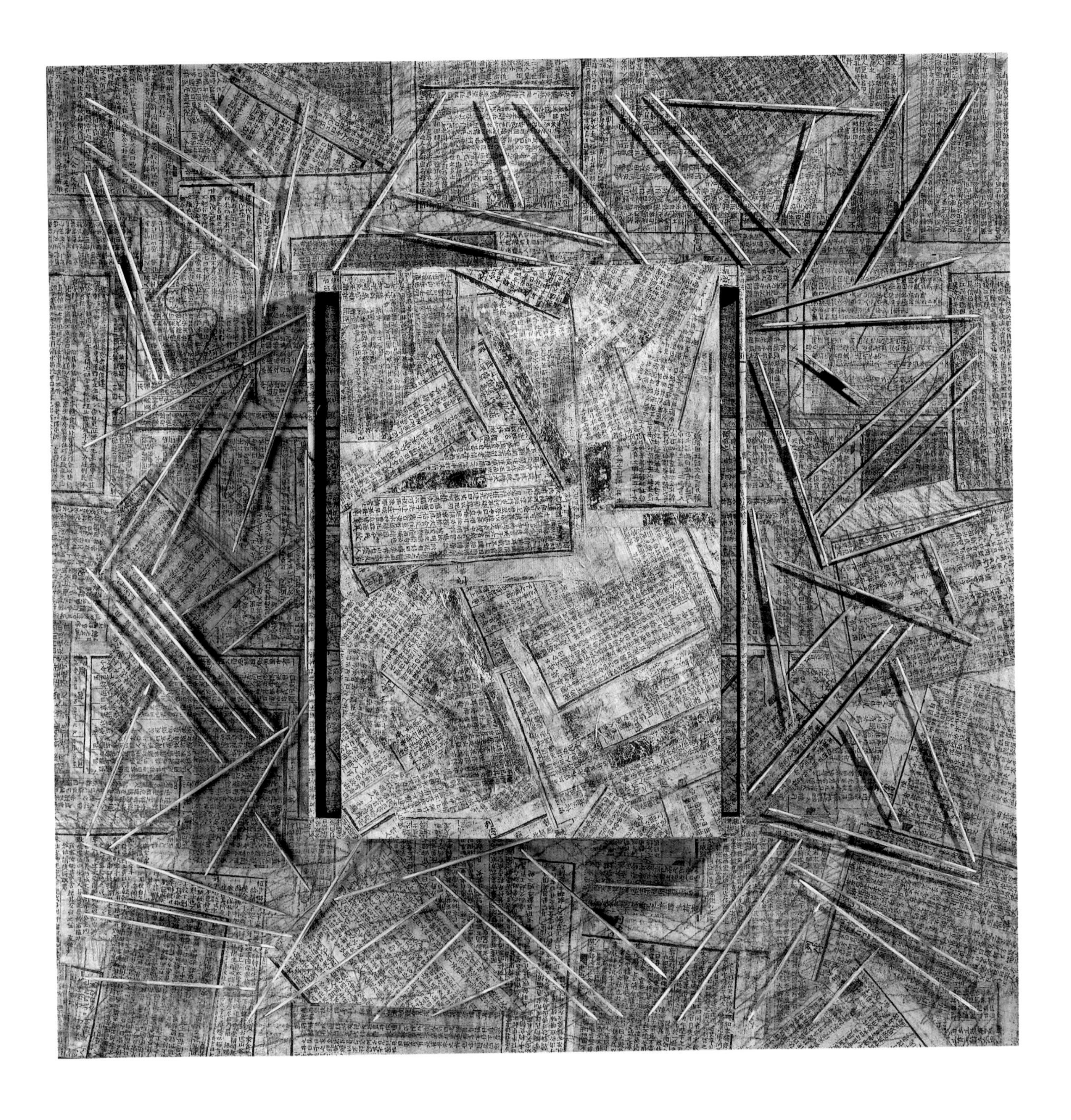

Old handmade Korean paper, bamboo, paint, 24 kt. gold foil, colored pencils, graphite, used fruit shipping crate

"The environment has become a social theater. . . . Colors, patterns, forms, textures, and most importantly, choice of materials can effectively counterbalance the plethora of microchip technology and standardized parts."

FRANKLIN D. ISRAEL DESIGN ASSOCIATES INC.

BEVERLY HILLS, CALIFORNIA

Franklin D. Israel

Photocopy of wood grain

"The materials of the future come from the imagination. . . .
Seeing the immediate world in different ways will help us select materials that best represent things as they are, and force us to understand better how precious are those things that . . . give us beauty, scale, and harmony."

IVY ROSS

SANTA MONICA, CALIFORNIA

Wood, steel wire, copper wire, plastic, grass

"There is no longer one society, but many societies.
Ways to express that individuality must be incorporated into the built environment.
It must be able to grow and change just as individuals do over time."

CENTRO DESIGN E COMUNICAZIONE S.R.L.

MILAN

Francesco Binfarè

Wood, canvas, plaster, pencil,

fiber resin, polyurethane paint,

printed paper

AD SA + PARTNERS

PARIS

Roger Tallon

Pear wood, cement with

aggregate stone, metal chips

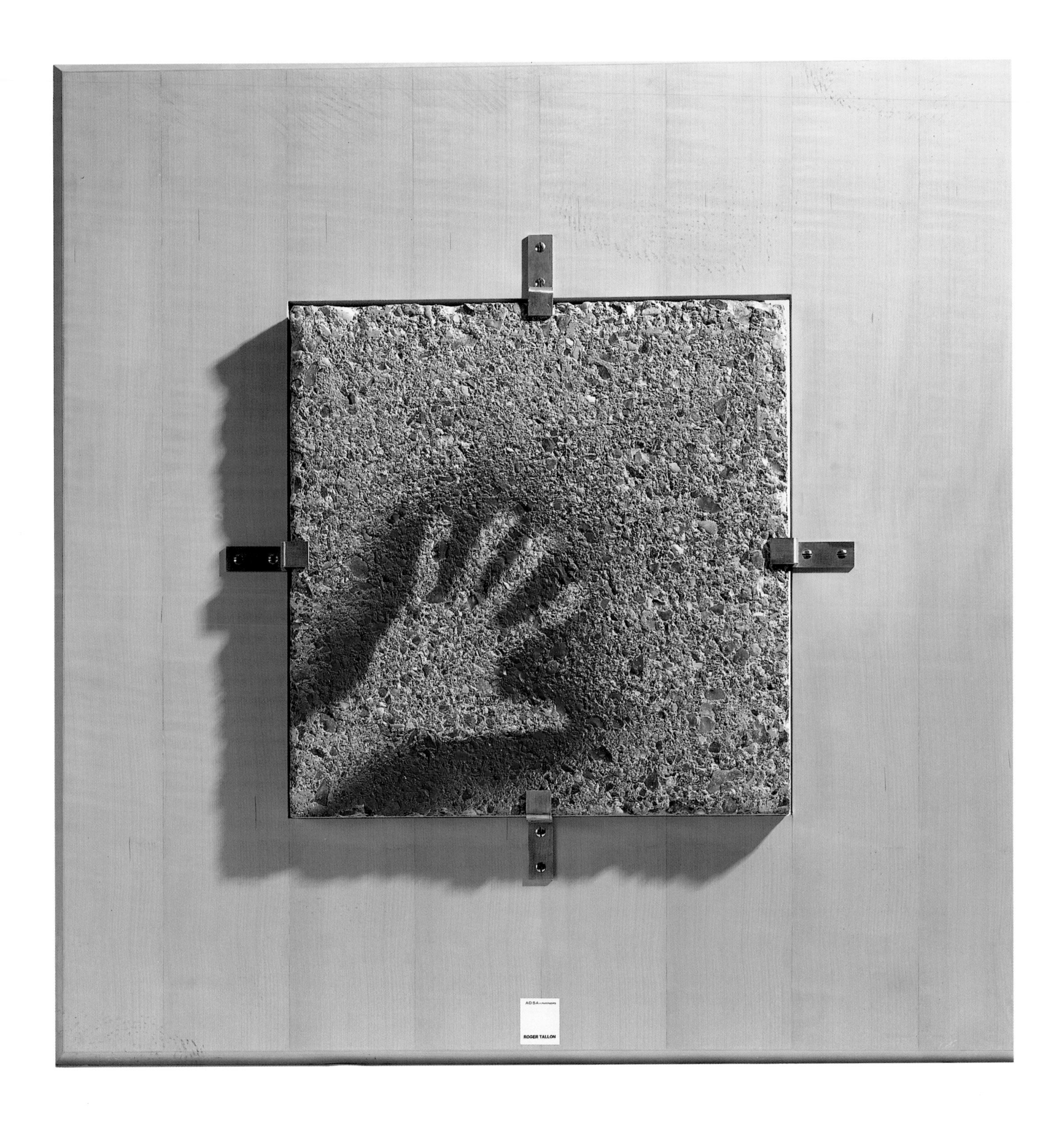

"Architecture will find its everlasting character from the authenticity of materials and its renewal from the technologies applied."

ATELIER DE PASCAL MOURGUE

PARIS

Pascal Mourgue

Glass, twigs

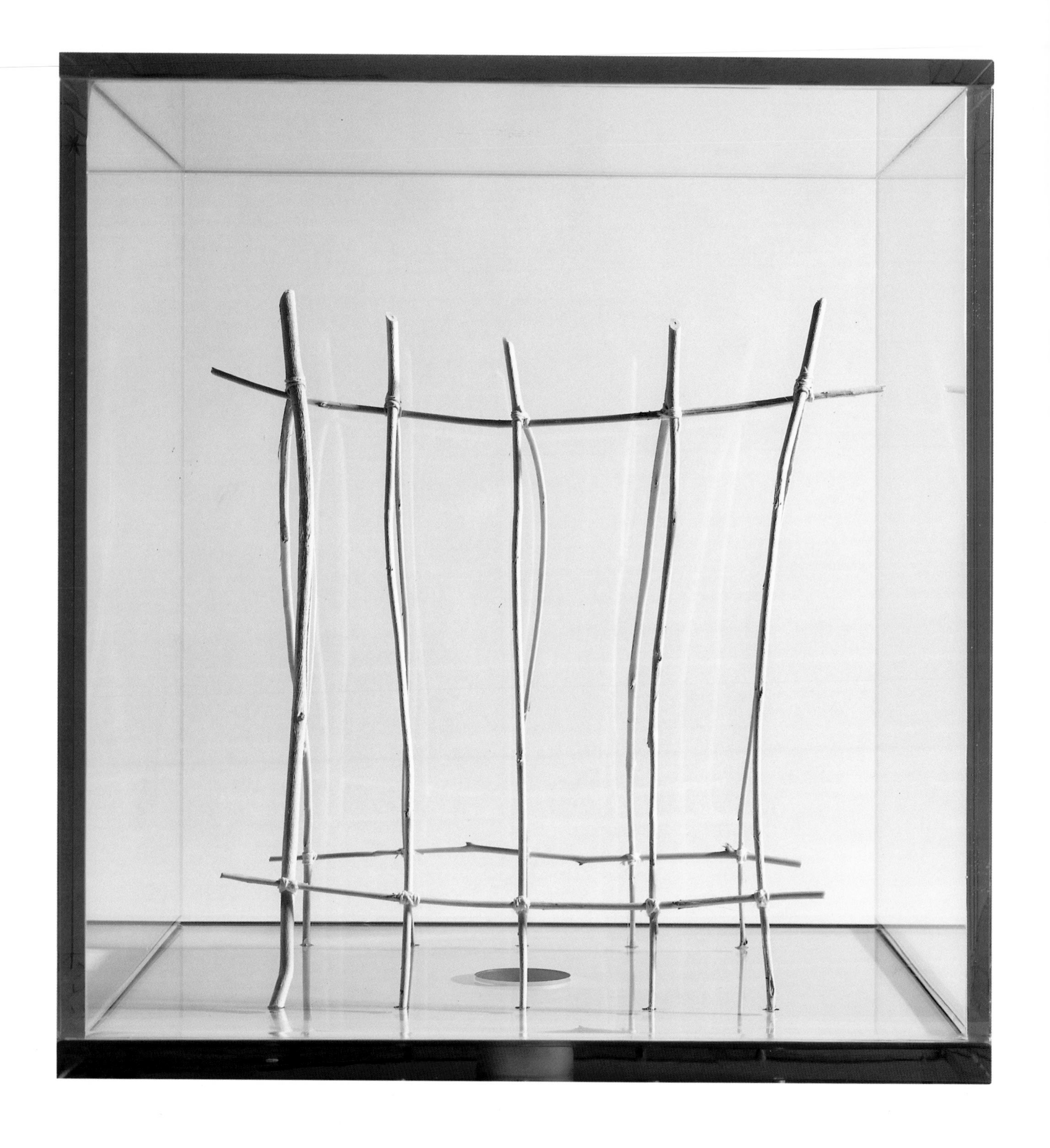

"It is by considering the intelligent use of the materials of the past that we will create the materials of the future."

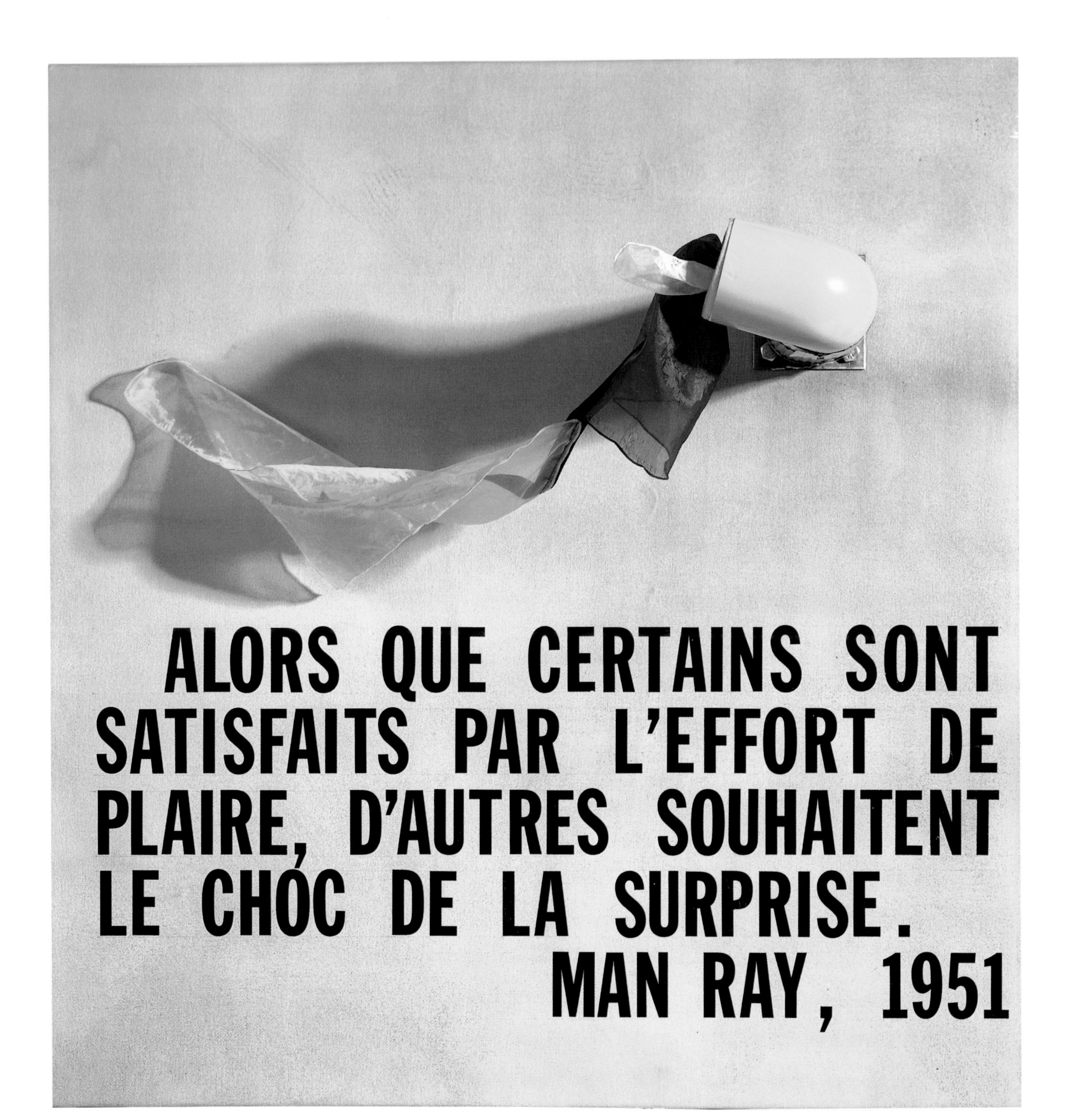

SAM LOPATA, INC.

NEW YORK

Barbara Pensoy, Sam Lopata

Silk scarves, angled metal, plastic

V. KIRPICHEV ASSOCIATION

MOSCOW

Vladislav I. Kirpichev

Nielloed steel, stainless steel, cuprite, red copper, brass, marble, gabbro, labradorite, fumed oak, rosewood, walnut, lemon wood, European wart birch, ebony, larch, glass, matte glass

"We must beware of reducing the goods found in our world into mere components for our workshops."

WILLIAM LIPSEY & ASSOCIATES/ ARCHITECTS

ASPEN, COLORADO

Bill Lipsey

Zinc, boards, peeled poles,

rubber flooring, silk, white paint

DAKOTA JACKSON, INC.

NEW YORK

Dakota Jackson

Paper, leather

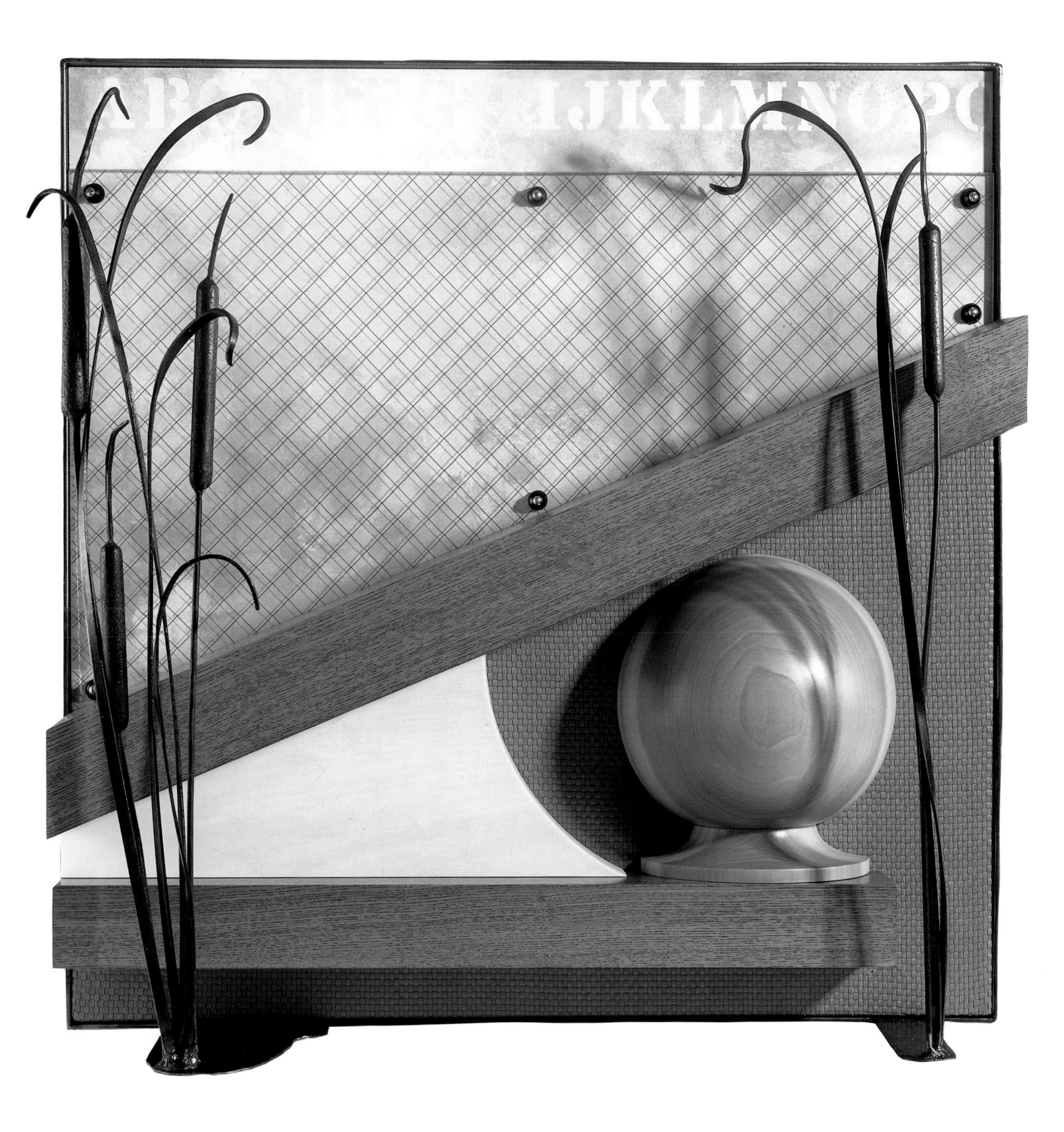

AGNES BOURNE, INC.

SAN FRANCISCO

Agnes Bourne

Iron cattails, stained woods, woven leather, upholstery, wire glass, hardware

LEWIS AND MICKLE STUDIO

NEW YORK

Diane Lewis;

studio team: Gerard Sullivan

Film stills

"The material challenge for the architect throughout history is to house the spirit."

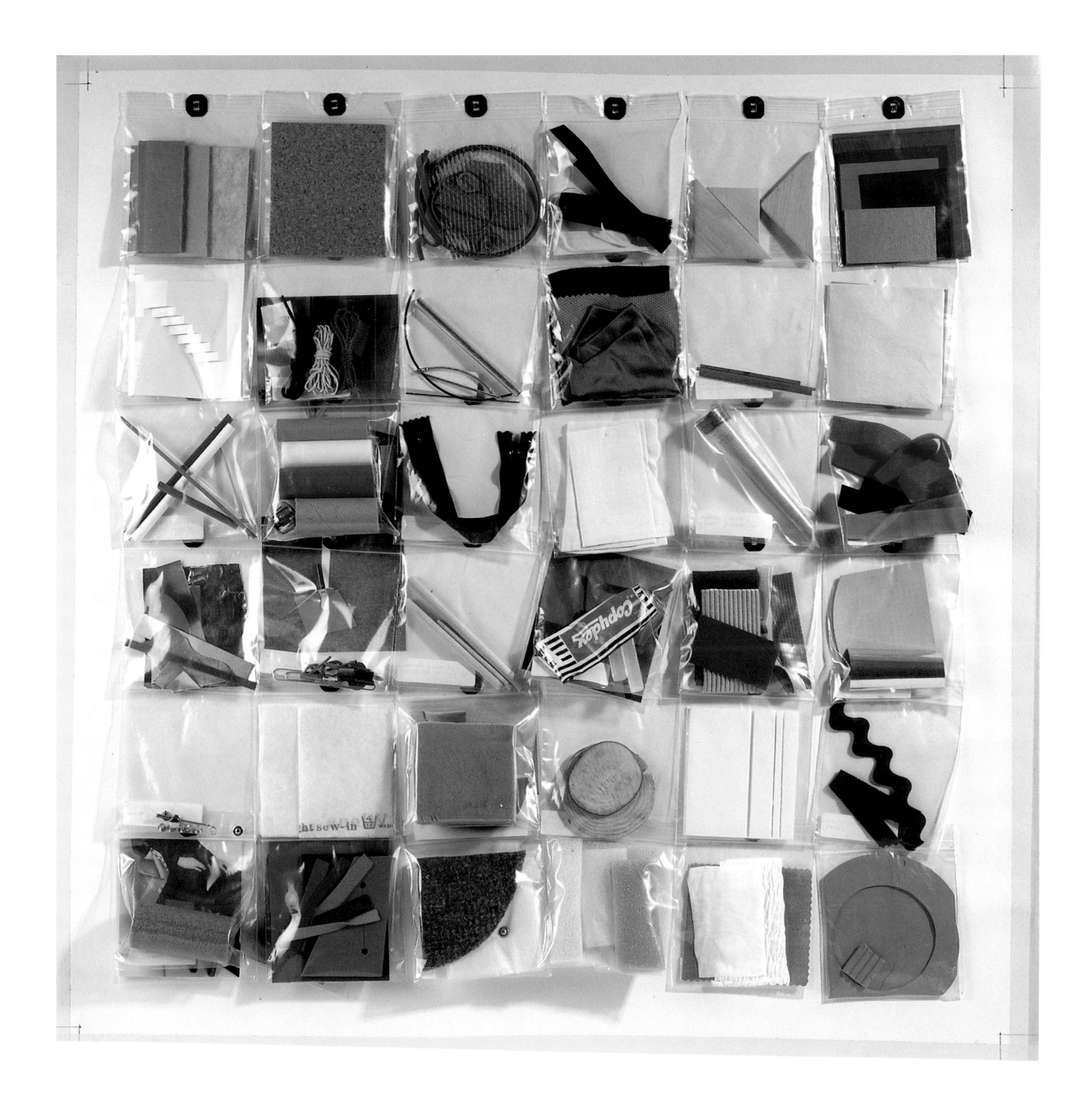

MARY LITTLE

LONDON

Studio samples

FITCH RS

LONDON

Rodney Fitch

Silkscreen print over wood veneer, metal, Plexiglas, paper, fabric, electronic components, wires

"The environmental crisis, growing consumer awareness and unrest, perhaps suggests a return to more natural materials and a more transparent design ethic."

MARIE-CHRISTINE DORNER ARCHITECTURE INTÉRIEURE—DESIGN

PARIS

Marie-Christine Dorner

Foam, wool, leather,

stained beech, bamboo,

copper, laminated steel

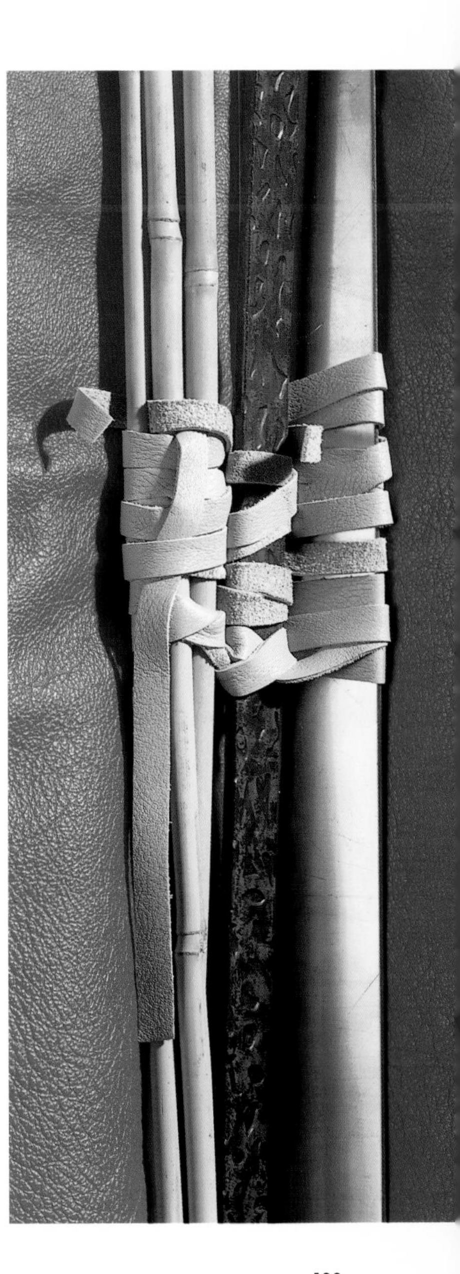

ROGER KRAFT: ARCHITECTURE-DESIGN

KANSAS CITY, MISSOURI

Roger Kraft, Designer;

Gentry Mullen, Project Coordinator

Maple — solid and veneer, matte board, colored paper, oil pastel, alkyd paint, glass

"The wood, glass, paper, drawing, and paint media used in my panel have been selected for their abilities to create a complementary set of formal and plastic incidents and points of emphasis within an overall structure and image. The orchestration transcends the material, as I think it should in matters of art and culture."

BERTHET-POCHY

PARIS

Jean-Louis Berthet

Light bulb, mirror, stone, wood, leather, wool

THE NINETIES : TWO KINDS OF MATERIALS
WILL CREATE OUR ENVIRONMENT

1. SHADOWS AND LIGHT

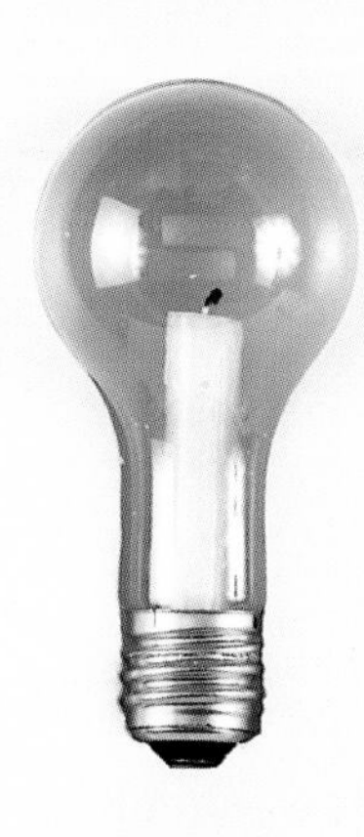

LIGHT IS A REAL ARCHITECTURAL ELEMENT
WHICH STRUCTURE SPACE, SHAPE UP VOLUMES
AND BOOST ENVIRONMENT

1. MIRROR AND REFLECTION

DREAMING YOUR SPACE WITH NEW PERSPECTIVES
"MIROLLEGE", HIGH TEMPERATURE
STRECHED FILM SURFACE UPON ALUMINIUM FRAME

2. TRADITION AND ACTUALITY: STONE, WOOD, LEATHER, WOOL

"The demand for quality and durability plays an integral role in the choice of materials, which also explains the return to natural and traditional materials."

GERE KAVANAUGH/DESIGNS

LOS ANGELES

Gere Kavanaugh

Tile,

wood/maple flitch,

faux cortin,

photograph on

white-coated

masonite

PAUL LUDICK

NEW YORK

Birch, plywood,

steel, canvas,

commercial globe

DETAILS

NEW YORK

David M. Gresham, James Ludwig

Cardboard with silver metallic finish

"Novel material innovations are certain to be the very stuff upon which the future will be built."

FITCH RICHARDSONSMITH +

COLUMBUS, OHIO

Matthew Hern, Jane Brady, John Rheinfrank

Urethane foam, pastels

GK INDUSTRIAL DESIGN ASSOCIATES

TOKYO

Kenji Ekuan

Graphics on photograph

Statements

Each of the *Mondo Materialis* participants was asked to contribute a statement along with their panel designs. The length—or brevity—of the statement and the subject was left to the discretion of the individual firm or designer. Some of the responses were pure whimsy and some entirely practical explanations; others were more considered philosophical musings about the nature of creativity, and more than a handful were inspired to write poetry. But whether the writings were specific or aesthetic, the overwhelming responses showed a serious concern for the future of the environment and a healthy and sensitive appreciation for the past. The statements have been arranged according to the sequence of the collage panels. In addition are statements by a number of architects and designers, whose work is not included here but who wished to contribute their thoughts about the nature of design today and in the future.

Torsten A. Fritze
San Francisco

In California, as well as when in Italy, I am constantly reminded of the fascinating effect that light has on the man-made environment. How the natural daylight enhances or distorts our perception of space and materials is altered by the changing conditions of illumination. As the day wears on, the direction or inclination of light changes, the weather changes, or we decide to switch on artificial sources; in each instance new aspects of materials are revealed.

The panels in this piece for *Mondo Materialis* reflect my fascination with light as a central, enhancing aspect of the environment. The Chinese Joss papers beautifully illustrate the qualities I most enjoy in materials. Color, contrast, reflection, transparence/opaqueness, and structure/texture—their individual positioning should allow for unique, subtle perceptions, caused by their different exposures to light. The cottage illustrates how a simple treatment can enhance and differentiate one material, how it can be used intelligently to simulate and express variety. It's these soft, man-made aspects that I believe are going to be the key element in the environment of the 90s. By "soft aspect" I intend the intelligent use of light and printed materials, laminates in combination with traditional materials to enrich the environment. My aim is the creation of a simple, almost spartan surrounding, which stimulates our senses without disturbing them.

Weber & Kalmes
Luxembourg

Weber & Kalmes is a young European designer-group based in Luxembourg. Our work consists mainly of interior design conception and execution. We also do sculptural projects for interior or exterior use. And finally, we are always searching for combinations of old and new materials to create a new dimension having properties that cannot otherwise be obtained using just one of the components.

Our panel is an example of sandblasted wood which has been covered by a patina-plated copper surface resulting in an electrical conductable medium. (Imagine wooden wires leading to a functioning light bulb.) Zinc, copper, aluminum, brass, bronze, and chrome combine this rich variation of surface finishes with the infinity of forms. We are using this technique to conceive large wall reliefs, decorative panels, three-dimensional sculptures, lighting fixtures, topographical maps, and so on.

Studio Sowden
Milan

Please find enclosed
some leaves.
There are
many natural
materials.
We hope
somehow
that our built environment
will remember
(not necessarily natural materials)
but
NATURE.
Thank-you.

Studio Nurmesniemi Ky
Helsinki
Antti A. Nurmesniemi

I made my panel out of wood wishing to show, with the use of a simple example, the strength of renewal that is continually found in natural materials. In this instance, I combined the material with a high level of craftsmanship.

Paolo Portoghesi ed Associati
Rome
Paolo Portoghesi

The creation of artificial materials over the last few decades has given us the illusion that it is possible to do without what for centuries has been the repertoire of forms and materials of architectural tradition. Now, however, events are taking place in our industrial society that have renewed the emphasis on the undying qualities of certain traditions. The energy crisis, the upsetting of the ecological balance, the destruction of the beauty of the countryside (especially in overpopulated regions of Europe), the need to build a peaceful civilization to replace one in conflict are all problems that can be labeled as "postmodern." This suggests that instead of considering a return to the past, we should consider the necessity of conserving and protecting our heritage from the past—in order, among other things, to serve as a permanent example to us. It is only right and proper that traditional materials should come back into our homes to symbolize solidity and durability, to add solemnity to family life, to bring into the home the image of nature and its endless variety. What indeed could be better than the veining of a fine piece of stone to recall the beauty of a landscape or of a cloudy sky? What could be better than the texture of the wood of a cypress or an olive tree to suggest "Genius Loci" in our homes?

Marble furnishings were a characteristic of ancient Rome, and had a great revival in the Renaissance and in the early nineteenth century. The time is right once more for revival of this local tradition, in forms which, though new, are faithful to the "Genius Loci." With this aim, we wanted to recall via the tabletops, the diametric inlay-work of the floors of ancient times, and the creative inspiration that was drawn from them by Borromini in the seventeenth century. And so another link is added in the chain that joins us to a city which found its symbol and its identity in eternity.

Michael McDonough, Architect
New York

The panel, an American flag image constructed from recycled cans, points to issues traditionally perceived as "outside of design"; that is, apart from important components of professional practice and materials technology in the 1990s. Its aluminum soda cans, cardboard, and vinyl adhesive caulk are quite common materials serving as indicators of uncommon problems. As much as they are part of our daily lives, or in the case of the caulk part of the construction industry, they are also reminders of solid waste, environmental, and other similar problems that will have continuing impact on design in the future. Aluminum cans are everywhere. Let us also remember that aluminum production is a highly energy-intensive and waste-water intensive process, and that the bauxite in aluminum comes primarily from developing countries—a reminder of north/south global political, environmental, and financial interdependence. Cardboard, seemingly benign, is also typical of the paper waste that constitutes well over half of all solid waste generated in the United States, and is a reminder of the global issues of deforestation and destruction of mature growth trees in American forests. Vinyl adhesive, used in new home and renovation projects, is typical of nonbiodegradable substances, from plastic bottles to baby diapers, that stay, often with destructive consequences, in the environment for years.

Smart Design, Inc.
New York

Wheel of Fortune

Today designers are positioned to play a vital role in the survival of the human race—indeed, of the whole planet. Industrial designers are the fortune tellers of their trade—they choose materials, foresee manufacturing processes, anticipate ergonomic, safety, and maintenance problems, and imagine disposal solutions. The future depends on the skill of the designer to find ways to protect society and the environment from technology that is unintentionally dangerous or carelessly wasted.

Nothing can be considered garbage anymore, for there is no longer any room or energy to squander. We hope to raise the appreciation of recyclable materials with this collage of materials collected by R2B2/Recoverable Resources, Bronx Boro 2000. Designers can specify this plastic, paper, and metal that is now piling up in collection sites all over the world. Ronald Reagan's (and James Watt's) trickle-down theory is working—it's dripping on us. We can no longer afford to throw anything away. The world is not going to get better until designers create sound products that consumers not only should use but want to use. The World of Tomorrow was conceived fifty years ago for the New York World's Fair. Now it is up to us to create a World with a Future.

Wood/Marsh
E. Melbourne, Australia

The work for this exhibition is an abstract representation of the architectural language that currently predominates in our work. Broadly, this deals with issues of geometry, perspective, convergence, and presence. Philosophically, these ideas will take our work further into the next decade. Physically, the exhibit sits on a topographical plane made from recycled plastic which is being developed in Australia for the building industry. Cutting through this is a blade of steel with an applied reflective coating which bisects one and passes another form constructed from high-density fiberboard. All these materials are precariously balanced between the environment and the future.

McCoy & McCoy
Bloomfield Hills, Michigan
Michael and Katherine McCoy

Im Material

Chopped foam is the material of the future with a past. Every scrap of foam and fabric has a history—its own texture, density, and color—which comes together quite accidentally as an assemblage at that moment when the block of detritus is pressed together. Chopped foam is the very embodiment of recycling, of taking cast-offs and making from them something new. It is one material that is enriched by the recycling process. Chopped foam is immaterial, nonmaterial, or every material: it is soft in texture, humble and comfortable, and it comes in all colors.

Padrós/Riart/Tió Mobles Casas
Barcelona
Carlos Riart LLOP

I believe that technological advances should be focused upon regenerating what has been bequeathed to us, the world in which we live, and upon a society that understands that the quality of life is in the richness of this globe and not merely in the comfort created by the conservative person.

Jonathan R. W. Teasdale
New York

The imagery that I employ commemorates man's rational ability to alter his environment according to what he values as being good for him. I select materials based on their ability to physically manifest this philosophy through references to man, the environment he controls, and what he builds.

Masayuki Kurokawa Architect & Associates
Tokyo

"Design" is an attempt to capture both the struggle and the cooperation between the meaning which the material itself implies and the meaning of the form which is given to the material.

Glass: Specific gravity 2.5

This material prevents the passage of all things except light. Its fragility is the reason for its beauty. Its image is one of "look, but don't touch" and can be as magical as Cinderella's slipper.

Lead: Specific gravity 11.35

The color of the rough Sea of Japan in winter. It is a soft metal. It is easily corroded. However, it has a most natural image because it is going to disappear as time goes by.

Water: Specific gravity 1.0

With the correct light water can be a mirror. It ripples when it feels wind, and in winter it moves from a liquid to a solid state. Like a reverse of the images of Salvador Dalí.

Titanium: Specific gravity 4.51

This metal is light but strong and has a metallic gray color. It is neither white nor black. It gives the impression of something caught between two opposites.

Aluminum: Specific gravity 2.7

The color of bright clouds and sky. As a substance given to images of whiteness and softness, it is suitable to an age of gentility.

Stainless steel: "MIRROR" Specific gravity 8.0

This metal almost generates its own light, and it has an image similar to that of water. We are reminded of Alice in Wonderland's mirror.

Bronze (Niiro): Specific gravity 8.5

The traditional process of working with bronze has three hundred years of history in Japan. It carries with it, however, an image of human ill will and earthiness.

Rubber: Specific gravity 1.4

This material is very elastic. It has a long, even slippery, history. Its color is the color of hell, and yet its touch is that of the skin.

Zinc: Specific gravity 7.1

Its color is gray. It is the symbol of "today" because its vagueness of color is as indescribable as the air.

Metropolitan Furniture Corporation
South San Francisco
Robert Arko

Due to resource, environmental, and related economic issues, natural materials are becoming increasingly elitist in application. More cost efficient man-made or man-modified material solutions are now used as substitutions and will play an ever-increasing role in years to come. Typically, while these materials often possess greater performance characteristics, they are often simply imitative or visually derived "two-dimensional" substances, lacking the inherent material integrity common to natural materials.

In my piece I have chosen materials that deal with these issues to some degree. Because of the inherent ecological problems surrounding completely synthetic materials, in particular nondegradable plastics, I have concentrated on man-modified materials which use renewable resources as their base.

Wood Flakeboard: Developed out of waste product decades ago, this very stable core material is recognized for its inherent visual qualities.

Linoleum: A relatively old material manufactured from the ultimate in renewable resources, cork, which is harvested as the bark of the Cork Oak. Though this material has been largely replaced by synthetic resilient flooring products, it is not matched for its material presence.

Recombined Wood Veneer: Although this product has also been around for some time, it has been used as a lower cost highly consistent replacement for traditional wood veneer. Developed for higher yields, it uses less exotic woods and, through a process of successive laminations, cuttings, and dyeing, achieves a very good approximation of natural wood. It has only fairly recently been developed to realize its own unique material qualities. The dark version is unfinished and integrally dyed, developing a graphite-like, blue-black linear quality which transcends its wood base. The second uses a slightly irregular pattern which has some of the dimensional qualities of exotically cut wood veneers, but considering the visual qualities and process of manufacture, suggests a hybrid veneer-textile.

Upholstery: The upholstered forms pay tribute to the fact that as a designer I spend a great deal of time working with upholstered forms. Though it is made up of a combination of both simple and advanced materials and technologies, in its final form the covering is only a part of the whole. The choice of the covering is sympathetic with the other materials used, in this case the processing and patterning over inherent imperfections.

Computer-Aided Manufacturing: It was my desire to recognize the technology that is and will continue to impact upon me as a designer. While providing me with new opportunities for processing materials, computer-aided manufacturing in particular is even more linked to the development of the material itself.

Eva Jiricna Architects
London

Materials can be processed and transformed from their natural state in many varied ways, depending on their own special characteristics. New materials can be developed to satisfy a new set of criteria, although their availability and relative cost depends on the supply and demand of many industries. As such, finished products marketed for the building industry are only a small proportion of those possible or available.

The materials selected for the exhibition show a full range of options, from natural stone to synthetic resin. Particular materials are chosen to provide solutions to particular problems. The selection of materials, then, and their processing demands a design language of its own in the way it is incorporated into the overall design.

Glass is a suspended liquid that is receptive to new technologies and can be transformed into a thinking manipulator of the environment; it will continue to be a major material of the future. Metals and alloys are constantly being developed, gaining new characteristics by their chemistry or production techniques. These will continue to expand. Natural materials have an endearing quality of their own. Stone or timber, for instance, can be used in sensitive ways to retain their inherent qualities. New materials on the other hand are an exciting development area that is less predictable: fabrics, resins, adhesives, etc., will all find their place in the built environment.

Hopefully research programs, industrial production, and imagination will work more in conjunction so that materials can be used in a sensible and creative fashion, with due consideration to function, quality of life, economy, and conservation.

Tom McHugh
Philadelphia, Pennsylvania

Materials, like color, are relative to their adjacent components, and ultimately to the space they occupy or create. In the nineties, economic conditions in the real estate market will result in much smaller rentable spaces, forcing designers to stretch the visual limits of these spaces. Also, with the advent of electrical components in advanced technology it will be necessary to counterbalance these spaces with more personal visual anchors. This counterbalancing can be achieved in many different ways: integration of nature (in a real or implied manner), stylized interruption of furniture with historical overtones (in a lighter manner with inherent patinas), a return to earth tones (with saturation of color yet clearer hues) and "candy apple" accents, recycling classic fabrics (Alexander Girard, c. 1960) and juxtaposing them with new-age materials to give them both a new vitality and personality. However, if one ignores the effect of materials on the environment, all this will be in vain and smothered in waste, as evident by the debris found on a twenty-minute stroll along the New Jersey shore.

Murphy/Jahn
Chicago
Nada Andric

Stones, woods, metals, wools, cottons, and silks will always be in my "Five Year Projections to the Future." I will use them indefinitely, but this is easy to predict. Along with these permanent choices, systematic high-tech solutions deriving from the technology of the moment will likewise be explored for appropriate applications.

The materials on our board are assembled as a response to the needs of interiors in public spaces, specifically those with high levels of traffic such as airports and train terminals. Here, well-known materials are articulated with surface treatment (fritting, etching, etc.), and given a new appearance and meaning.

Sumform
Long Island City, New York
William Schiffman

The materials on my panel represent a prominent but incomplete palette which I like, need, and use as an industrial designer. In the next five years technology will continue to develop new materials and new applications of these materials. Consumers will become increasingly aware of quality materials and good design. I will still begin with graphite and paper, consider a vast array of materials available to fit function, aesthetic, and production method constraints and then use capital to make dreams a reality.

Kawakami Design Room
Tokyo
Motomi Kawakami

Human beings are linked to the diverse elements of nature, either through the forms that nature itself creates or through synthetic materials fashioned from these elements by means of technology. The task of the designer is to use his powers of description and representation to give meaning to these materials.

In my work I combine natural wood and stone with modern synthetic materials to create designs suited to specific purposes and locations. For this panel, I have used a variety of materials to create a likeness to the image of mandala.

David Zelman
New York

I work primarily in steel, and most of my work is inspired by the machine and other technological advances of the industrial age. Some of the crucial aspects on which my work focuses are structure, monumentality, tension, balance, and human achievement.

Studio De Lucchi
Milan
Michele De Lucchi

The problem with new materials is not the materials: that is, I do not believe it is necessary to search for anything more than cement, stone, marble, ceramics, plastics, polyurethanes, rubber, textiles, laminates, etc. The problem with new materials is that of allowing them to speak a new language: just as, in the eighties, we used laminate, and we decorated, designed, and utilized it in unusual places, thus transforming a poor and common material into a rich and noble one.

Now that there is much sensitivity concerning the safeguarding of nature, attempts will be made to understand whether it is better to use plastics and to control their uses and abuses, or to use natural materials and try to avoid their abuse. In order to allow materials to express themselves in new languages, we must communicate sensations that are more emotive, and, I hope, that will also be happier and more optimistic.

Decor will surely be of great assistance, because decor is still a new issue—the current conception of decor actually emerged during the eighties, not more than ten years ago. Moreover, a new material can also be a projection of a new decor or a new image constructed out of many old forms of decor designed during the course of the preceding decade.

Coop Himmelblau
Vienna • Los Angeles
West Los Angeles, California

Steel and Glass are Materials Which are Made with Fire

Steelcase Inc.
Grand Rapids, Michigan

The materials used in this collage are from a new collection developed specifically for Context, the new Steelcase Systems Furniture. The finishes were selected to celebrate one another and to show how well they work together. The Melange coating is a speckled multicolor finish designed to coordinate with a variety of different materials, textures, and colors. The Mono-Tex finish is a textured paint with a new color line. Caldera coating is designed to simulate a distressed metal look. Silque is a new coating developed for work surfaces. This matte finish reduces eye strain and the coating gives surfaces a wonderful smooth hand. Altissima is a panel fabric line with a high-tech rib texture and an iridescent dimensional quality. Dimity is a panel fabric line in a classic pattern. Selene is a new silk tweed multicolor panel fabric. Mordezza is a panel fabric line in subtle two-tone colorations. These materials were developed to be used together. They were created to respond to market needs for multicolored, textured finishes, and the ability to play different kinds of finishes off one another. The textiles were developed to be used together or separately. The color lines were designed to be compatible.

Ross Lovegrove
London

Because I am a product and furniture designer, my exhibit presents a variety of materials in colors and tactile finishes that currently relate to small objects and which, in my view, could equally be translated into the composition of interiors and architecture. These samples continue to inspire me to combine materials, through their simple visual and functional juxtaposition, that hopefully express a fresh confidence and modern sensuality.

In the way that a beautiful piece of architecture needs a landscape or a setting to express its true character, small volumes of material, which interface directly with us, require a deeper perspective and a more valuable examination rather than being tossed away as obsolete or as infinitely replenishable.

The Richard Penney Group
New York

Materials are the Palette of Our Ideas

In the coming generation, we intend to use the vocabulary of materials and finishes both singularly and juxtaposed in architectural spaces, and as an integral part of furniture and products. Elements of surface, form, and detail will emerge. By design, our materials will bring both simplicity and complexity to our work. With appropriateness and cost-effectiveness we will impart an aesthetic that reflects our emotional intervention, vitality, and hand. These vital elements will convey a spirit that is at once familiar and unexpected to the context of production and built environments. Searching tradition and today's possibilities, we find a reverence and truth in these materials, processes, and craft. They are elements of our cultural and technological language.

Able
New York

when serpents bargain for the right to squirm
and the sun strikes to gain a living wage—
when thorns regard their roses with alarm
and rainbows are insured against old age

when every thrush may sing no new moon in
if all screech-owls have not okayed his voice
—and any wave signs on the dotted line
or else an ocean is compelled to close

when the oak begs permission of the birch
to make an acorn—valleys accuse their
mountains of having altitude—and march
denounces april as a saboteur

then we'll believe in that incredible
unanimal mankind (and not until)

e.e. cummings

Walz Design
New York

Little of our existence has shown such lack of reconsideration through the frantic twentieth century than our perception of quality in building materials, which is still that of the nineteenth century. There is irony in our desperation to work with those materials, now rare and costly, that are called natural. We feel more soothed being in an environment with these materials no matter how superficially they are deployed. One thirty-second of an inch of rain forest mahogany over humble plywood or particle board, or one-quarter inch of granite laminated to a corrugated aluminum structure convey our attempts to hold on to this antiquated vision of quality.

We need to come to the realization that what our world really is constructed of frequently lies just below the surface. These materials have just as much structural and visual integrity as those materials that we can no longer responsibly deplete from the world at such a rapid rate. It is the role of the designer to find new uses for these materials of inherent integrity that we repeatedly veneer and laminate. It is also the role of the designer to educate the public and industry about redefining their perceptions of quality materials. We do not need to abandon all natural materials and methods, but we do need to leave our natural resources in balance by integrating more of the materials that are truly a part of our time. This way, our solutions will be more appropriate to the realities of the end of the twentieth century.

PHH Environments
Los Angeles
Rinaldo Veseliza

The materials represented on our whimsical board are both natural and man-made, which I believe will be the direction of our design concepts over the next five years.

As our society becomes so much more involved with computers and microchips, which we cannot really see or touch, our personal and work environments will require more tactile, sensually stimulating materials to help us, as natural, living creatures, become in touch with our organic selves. This board represents the man-made materials with which we will continue to construct our world. The plastic wonders of Corian-type materials, the plastic laminates, and the synthetic fibers are here to stay. I envision the clarity and purity of colors reemerging in the next five years. Of course, the metallic colors are becoming the "hot" items in architecture, furniture, and fabric design. Reflective qualities of metals are spreading to fabrics, paints, and color concepts for interior design projects. I believe this is a reflection of not only our technological advances in space, but a reconfirmation of our dependence on man-made materials, as well as a growing shortage of natural materials. Natural materials, however, are being reproduced with extraordinary skill. Exotic leathers are being copied using sophisticated manufacturing techniques. With wood veneers, it is difficult to distinguish the type of wood used in large-production wood products. Nothing is what it appears to be, and much of it is fabricated from reconstituted material. Everything looks "regular" and uniform. I believe this trend will make the natural, irregular, one-of-a-kind wood product very rare indeed. In fact, this will lead the design community to appreciate the irregularity found in antiques and the individuality found in the crafts and fine arts.

The board itself represents the philosophy of design which is changing so rapidly between the Post-modern and Deconstructionist/Deconstructivist (or called "decon") movements as we head into the New Age where the world is becoming one vast design marketplace. American designers are working in Asia; Japanese and Chinese designers are working in the United States; and Europe is becoming united as one large state. The world is shrinking and our greatest resource is humanity. How we assemble these materials will be determined by our ingenuity.

Haigh Space Architects/Designers
Greenwich, Connecticut
Paul Haigh and Barbara H. Haigh

Five Memos for the Material World

With a nod toward Italo Calvino's *Six Memos for the Next Millennium,* this submission identifies some material values applicable to our work.

TRUTH
RHYTHM
PERCEPTION
COHERENCE
LEVITY

These values form the ideological basis from which our material selections initiate.

King-Miranda Associati
Milan

All materials are also three-dimensional volumes, a part of man's work. These materials and their treatment are one answer to the needs of people everywhere—in their work place or in their home, and for an artificial or built world, which is related to the natural world.

Andrea Branzi Architetto
Milan

I'm interested in these materials because they have a "double soul." From one side, they are man-made materials that have become "classics," as if they were a second nature. From the other side, they are natural materials that have become similar to the man-made ones. Artifice follows nature, although nature too imitates artifice.

CDM Castelli Design Milano s.r.l.
Milan
Clino Trini Castelli

The title of this work is "cultured wood," an allusion to pearl growth. I find the ambiguity of this natural/unnatural material and its relationship to the color requirements of the present and immediate future of particular significance. While this product is first and foremost a flooring material, I do foresee its use in a wide range of other applications throughout the whole field of interior design.

M. W. Steele Group, Inc.
San Diego

Building on a base of strength and continuity, we will experience a world in the 1990s where emphasis is placed on traditional human values and freedom.

Copper, a pure and timeless material largely unspoiled by trends, was chosen to express the basic traditional values expected to be the common building-block of future societies. Our piece explores a variety of forms of this single material. The clear strength of the base serves to support a complex, sensuous form at the core. The copper rods supporting this core serve to lace the composition together. The execution expresses simplicity of thought resulting in complexity of form.

Danny Lane
London

The walls do speak, we have only to listen. The potency of *material* is derived from more than stress factors and scientific coding alone. Manufacturing often seeks uniformity to benefit repetitive effects. These materials are of different natures and have already lived different lives.

nob + non
New York

The concept of "earth" represents
a universal material which contains
sensibility
integrity
harmony
essence.

A+O Studio
San Francisco
Aura Oslapas

The microchip can execute functions within nanoseconds. Speed and power are continually expanding. Our clients barrage us with the products of the electronic, information age—words. It is becoming difficult to focus and delve into our work as more and more information arrives that requires reading, discussion, responses. Technology beckons constantly, removes the tactile nature of materials, and shifts us into a realm of words and simulation. Although we hesitate to share the creative process with technology, we yearn for it to shorten the more mundane tasks to be performed. Throughout all this, we hang on to our craft tools, the materials of our creative process. These are the materials of our ideas—we touch and squeeze them, chew on them, and transform them as we use them up.

Casson Mann Designers
London
Dinah Casson, Roger Mann

Our vision of "the built environment of the next five years" is one dominated by instruments of communication. The television screen, in our view, will be one of the most important of these, not only as a broadcaster of programs and information, but as a close-circuit eye. In this context the texture and quality of light a monitor produces create a new type of "material," with the precise image becoming irrelevant.

The hedge in our panel is not intended only as a simple statement of Green. Plastic, which can be recycled, will be the material of the future. Here, in its friendliest form, it contrasts with the rusted fragments of the industrial age, which we can no longer support.

ID TWO
San Francisco
Naoto Fukasawa

I enjoy this plastic material because of its color and lively pattern. This plastic is a rare example of a synthetic material because it has some of the random and accidental qualities of natural materials, such as wood or ceramic. It is not a new material—we are all familiar with it through its use in the eyewear frame industry. But in the same way that a new color can be created by combining several familiar colors, we can create designs that are fresh and surprising by using familiar materials in new applications or in new combinations with other familiar materials.

Artorium Inc.
Montreal, Quebec

Matter of Circumstance

An eye-catching sample of material for *Mondo Materialis,* the exhibition and book . . .

This material is an inexpensive floor covering,
easy to assemble,
fatigue-resistant,
antislip,
waterproof,
lightweight,
easily cleaned.
It can be cut to fit corners.
Available in different colors for color schemes.

The ping pong balls are the flaws. . . .

Pui-Pui Li & Eric Jones
Staten Island, New York

The title of our piece is "Internal Architecture," a term which refers to the physical structure of electronic and computing devices. We have envisioned the built environment coming to life, as artificial intelligence becomes fully integrated with structural elements. Even surface materials can become components in a larger electronic organism. Our materials are silicon computer chips, electronic circuit boards, PVC, and expanded aluminum.

Dan Chelsea Design
New York

To build boats, technology has historically used materials and structural applications that seemed in advance of the needs of most other building disciplines. I suspect that this occurs because the end user has a more active role in the process, typically to the point of obsession. The abundance of fertile ideas in boat-building makes for some terrific applications elsewhere.

The materials used to make the panel itself, and the items attached to it, represent some of the latest thinking in making boats. They share the common characteristics of altering incredibly weak material into something very strong and useful.

Syndesis, Inc.
Santa Monica, California
David Hertz, Stacy Fong, Susan Frank

Our submission primarily reflects the innovative use of Syndecrete™, a lightweight concrete that we have developed. Syndecrete™ can be integrally pigmented in any color, adopt the surface of the mold in which it is used, and be mixed with an infinite variety of aggregates. It is tooled with regular wood-working tools. Syndecrete™ has been used primarily as an architectural surfacing material. Its applications include countertops, tiles and wall panels, as well as cast sink basins, bathtubs, showers, and furniture.

It is our intention to explore the honest nature of raw materials and to exhibit the expressive quality of their processes of manufacture and fabrication. The black Syndecrete™ is used as the matrix in which the other materials are cast. This panel represents a cross section of materials as found in our recent work in art, architecture, furniture, and design.

Nederlandse Philips Bedrijven B.V.
Eindhoven, The Netherlands

Aurora

It is up to us to express technology. We can make it new or expressive through the use of materials. We can express the symbiotic relationship of elements that are both interdependent and work together, such as the earth, sky, light, sound, hot and cold. The tension between natural materials and high-tech materials, craft, and industry can be demonstrated.

A symbiosis exists between materials and culture. No one material dominates, for the choice is ours.

People are participants. The box can be opened, their curiosity rewarded.

In sound and light there is music and fantasy. Music has humanity, light is magnificent.

James Hong Design
New York
James Hong

Glass is a material used since ancient times. It is, however, always exciting to consider it as a "new" material. With this approach it is possible to see in it new possibilities. The panel provided here is a sample of a wall used in a bathroom. With the use of glass chips, it becomes translucent and decorative.

Pei, Cobb, Freed & Partners
New York

2 Man-made Materials

One, 3000 years old and still used
in its timeless beauty,
the other, a material invented yesterday,
made possible through space-age technology.

Both materials in themselves are timeless.
Only in the hands of the designer do these
materials come to life.

Donovan and Green
New York

New processes yield new materials. Translucency. Transparency. Color. Reflection. That which appears simple becomes complex on closer inspection. We no longer know what we are observing at first glance. The future is filled with materials that challenge the designer to explore and arrive at the unexpected. The dichroic filters are made by applying alternate layers of silicone dioxide and titanium dioxide to a high-temperature glass substrate. There are between seven and fifteen individual layers built up on the glass, each of which is the thickness of a wavelength. The spacing of the layers creates a different index of refraction for these filters than for clear glass. As a result, light is refracted differently and causes interference at various points of the visible light spectrum, depending on the number of layers. This is what gives the filters the appearance of having an integral color, even though the substrate and the silicone and titanium dioxide layers are inherently clear. As the viewing angle changes, the apparent filter color changes because the angle of refraction is also changing, thereby affecting the portion of the visible light spectrum seen.

Kozo Design Studio Inc.
Tokyo
Kozo Sato

I selected high-technological products as the materials to create my panel. For example, a small floppy disk for a computer, a luminous electric panel, a small answering machine. . . . Moreover, these high-tech products are important materials for use as other basic materials. I hope that we will find a better method to produce highly technological products to suit a pollution-free environment in the next five years.

Vent Design Associates
Campbell, California

These polymer materials represent the vast manipulation that man can have over the performance, shaping, and texturing of objects. As technology progresses there is more capability (quality, integrity, longevity) with objects if designed and manufactured correctly. Plastics, for instance, can lose their "cheap wrap" image; once recycled, they will not pollute the earth and, being a relatively limited resource, can be utilized more and more to that effect.

Associates & Ferren
Wainscott, New York

This is an I-Beam (or rather, an Eye-Beam). It is a prototype of a display case that reveals its contents to the viewer as they reveal themselves to it.

Our plan for the future is to create designs incorporating active materials that react dynamically to the environment and the viewer. You are invited to explore the dimensions of the ultrasonic sonar beam extending from the front of the orange ring. It hums because it does not know the words. Sorry. . . .

FTL Associates
New York

FTL believes in an architecture that emphasizes the integration of building systems through the use of a variety of fabrics and lightweight materials. Architecture is not a series of parallel processes. It is an integrated process that deals with all the elements at the same time. FTL maximizes the use of fabrics and lightweight materials by producing an architecture that integrates structure, lighting, and acoustics.

Our projects are designed with the idea that one can improve the built environment by the most economical means, yet minimize the impact on the natural environment.

Denis Santachiara
Milan

I selected these materials because they are not materials, but immaterials. They produce performances, and they change themselves with human contact.

William McDonough Architects
New York
William McDonough

William McDonough Architects has no fixed palette of materials; we are constantly reviewing new materials and methods for their potential use in projects. We employ a wide and somewhat eclectic collection of materials and techniques which range widely in cost, from completely custom to off-the-shelf. Often these extremes are combined. Some of the fundamental principles guiding our materials selection are as follows:

1. Materials are used to articulate the elements of the architectural composition. We often conceive of walls and surfaces as "objects" and coordinate material selection with detailing to enhance this reading.
2. An initial range of materials is selected to respond to long-term functional and aesthetic goals, and we use as low maintenance and as durable materials as budgets will allow.
3. Special consideration is afforded materials which are renewable, recyclable, or recycled. For our Paul Stuart project, we arranged for the planting of 1000 English Brown Oak trees.
4. We avoid materials potentially detrimental to the local and global environment and try to mitigate any negative ecological effects of our projects. Where possible, we specify substitutes for all materials containing formaldehyde or chlorofluorocarbons or other outgassing chemicals (found in glues, insulations, and paints, etc.) and do not use mahogany or other rain-forest woods. In the case of our seventy-story Warsaw project, a ten-square-mile forest outside the city is planned to help balance the project spatially, programmatically (recreation, land conservation), and environmentally.
5. We research locally available materials. For a ranch house in southern Utah we opened a quarry and built walls from local sandstone. Elsewhere we use dolomitic limestone from Minnesota and indigenous woods.
6. We seek out materials that exhibit the character of the craftsperson's hand, such as hand-planed woods and joinery, interference paints, fresco plaster, etc.
7. We allow poetic concerns to enter the discussion when selecting our palette of materials. Sometimes this will have a major impact on the form of the design: the Quilted Giraffe Restaurant is conceived as a crystalline "geode" of white metals within the granite AT&T Building. Sometimes it provides a subtle underlying message: the Warsaw Trade Center design calls for the tower to rise Phoenix-like from the center of the city.
8. Living material is considered at the same time as the building. In some cases specific plantings are integrated into the design. Indoor planting is incorporated for a sense of the outdoors and air purification. A specific tree outside a window is carefully composed for shape, color, and seasonal shading.

We are presently continuing our materials research in various areas such as the continued examination of the use of interference finishes, dichromatic glass and custom safety glass laminations (e.g., silk), metal fabrics for layered readings (see panel), the use of computer imaging transferred to laser-cutting technology for fine metal cutting and patterning, and the never-ending search for environmentally sound substitutes for conventional materials.

Zebra Design Inc.
New York

Hidden Exposure

Medium-density fiberboard is usually underneath laminates and veneers.

We like its beauty.

MDF is inexpensive.

We like to treat inexpensive things in more precious ways.

MDF is two-dimensional.

We like to make it three-dimensional through industrial processes such as carving, grooving, and molding.

MDF is an artificial material.

We like the patina that artificial materials acquire when they are left out.

Zebra Design.

We like to expose what is normally hidden.

Sottsass Associati
Milan

Contemporary Woods
Old—New
Traditional—Innovative
Natural—Artificial

The pendulum of taste and dialectics in design swings back and forth perpetually without ever reaching the perfect solution: an ideal compromise that embraces each of these values.

This panel—made of wood veneers and produced by Alpi of Modigliana—is something like a metaphor for these dialectics. The raw material for the veneer is wood, which is as old as the world, but the structure of the veins is totally artificial, identical sheet after sheet, as required by the industrial demands that it was developed to meet. Also, the colors are artificial. They are modern and updated to suit the trends of the next season, and absolutely constant. The frame, however, is made of natural pear wood and serves as an example of a wood becoming extinct, probably cut down on some sloping field on the banks of Lake Lucerne, having seen many daybreaks and many romantic sunsets against a background of snow-covered mountains.

Arquitectonica International Corporation
Coral Gables, Florida
Laurinda Spear

For the nineties, we feel that everything is possible. We like to use a combination of man-made and natural materials. We think that materials should biodegrade and be environmentally safe. In the nineties, extravagance feels inappropriate. We want to use straightforward, functional, affordable materials in new ways.

The Whitney Group, Inc.
Houston

Glass... an enigmatic and provocative material that has challenged designers and architects for centuries. Bountiful, yet rare... solid, yet transparent... structural, yet translucent... opaque or colored. We are beginning to challenge this wonderful material and the myriad of properties that we can bestow upon this child of sand. Our panel taps only a few of its endless possibilities. We show welded glass without traditional fasteners, an expression of planes and edges, a game board playing technical precision against old world craftsmanship. Most of all, ours is a celebration of light!

Vanderbyl Design
San Francisco
Michael Vanderbyl

I believe the future will see the exploration of humble "ordinary" materials and through their manipulation heighten their combined effect to a more noble aesthetic.

Jeffrey Beers Architects
New York
Jeffrey Beers

This panel represents an array of different finishes and forms that can be achieved with glass and metal materials. Great strides have occurred recently in these two industries that now allow limitless possibilities for design and construction. These two materials still appear to be evolving from a technological standpoint, and the 1990s look to be very exciting times for innovation and construction applications. Perhaps the most distinctive quality of these two materials lies in their inherent natural properties. The ability to alter, change, and adapt to different conditions and requirements makes metal and glass extremely versatile and attractive materials.

Dennis Oppenheim
New York

Objects chosen for photography. Photo-silkscreens prepared. Objects printed onto fabric. Ideally, the objects chosen would be in close proximity to their images printed on the fabric.

Richard Meier & Partners
Los Angeles/New York
Richard Meier

White is in fact the color which intensifies the perception of all the other hues that exist in natural light and in nature. It is against a white surface that one best appreciates the play of light and shadow, solids and voids. For this reason white has traditionally been taken as a symbol of purity and clarity, of perfection. Where other colors have relative values dependent upon their context, white retains its absoluteness. Yet when white is alone, it is never just white, but almost always some color that is itself being transformed by light and by everything changing in the sky, the clouds, the sun, the moon. Goethe said, "Color is the pain of light." Whiteness, perhaps, is the memory and the anticipation of color.

This submission to the "Mondo Materialis" exhibition represents a continued fascination with whiteness as a characteristic of my work. The nine squares show a range of varied reflectances from a dead flat through a high gloss. These finishes, combined with their exterior or interior application, affect the relative absoluteness of the white. Dead flat stands at the most absolute end of this spectrum. Its lack of reflection makes its wearer more of a solid, yet it still suggests the color and intensity of its surroundings. High gloss holds the least absolute qualities. Its more literal reflections of context give its surfaces a chameleon-like quality. These finishes offer me an added tool which I use in modulating the links between my work and its natural context.

Orlando Diaz-Azcuy Designs
San Francisco
Orlando Diaz-Azcuy

Because of the availability of finishing materials on the market, it is rare that designers concern or direct their attention to creating new ones. Most of the materials are here; it all depends how one uses them. Integrating the finishes as a total expression of the architecture and even expanding its visual and tactile quality is a direction in which I am constantly experimenting, and of late, with stronger effort. Using very simple common materials, objects, etc., to achieve effects beyond the individual properties for which they are normally intended, like nails on a surface in a desired pattern, is of great interest to me. I hope this panel illustrates one of the multiple possibilities.

Rogers and Goffigon Ltd.
Greenwich, Connecticut

This collection represents the best in natural fibers and classic design in both handwoven and power-woven textiles.

Thun Design
Milan
Matteo Thun

The idea is to use high-tech materials that have a natural look. This means porosity, glass, various materials in their original colors, aluminum having a three-dimensional appearance, and lacquers that are similar to aluminum behind glass. The gold centerpiece is a reminder of "old" Europe—the mosaics in Ravenna, the tilework in San Marco in Venice. Some of the materials in this panel were chosen by chance, and all have been used for two years in various point-of-sale chain stores as well as being elements in the industrial construction of facades.

Ricardo Bofill
Taller De Arquitectura
Paris
Annabelle d'Huart

These materials describe an ethereal aesthetic, one which strives to clarify the space, not cover it. It is a celebration of defined architectural volumes. The colors are generally muted, with an occasional outburst of color as an unexpected nuance. The onlooker is drawn into a meditative conversation, one which engages his spirit in a poetic dialogue with the world around him.

The textures Annabelle has created are quietly deductive but always present. They neither overwhelm nor bombard the onlooker with superfluous detail—instinctively, they pacify.

The aesthetic of the nineties will concern sensitivity; our hope is to employ materials that will enhance this interior state. Clarity, beauty, proportion: it is these ideals we strive to interpret in our spaces.

Martine Bedin
Milan

The materials with which one should build the world?

The materials with which one should build the future?

Those materials are the materials of the kings, and it cannot be otherwise, even though those who construct the world with anything less than stones are too modest. My materials are the materials of the kings and emperors, lords and princesses. In a way, marble, wood, slate, gold, and silver are the materials and colors of dreams.

Peter Stathis/Scott Zukowski
New York/Indianapolis

Truth is no longer stranger than fiction—truth is fiction.

Torck-Noirot
Paris

We prefer to emphasize the tactile sensation often left out of modern design. We surround the products we create with a bit of mystery so that a bond is created between the object and the client. Going against the typical "sober and impersonal" styles of modern furniture, we have chosen a warm environment to ensure that the day-to-day world becomes agreeable. We work on new functions, influenced by changing life-styles. We design furniture that lets itself be manipulated, that can change purpose, that lives.

Eric Owen Moss—Architect
Culver City, California

Chaired

Behind veneer,
peer;
Under wood,
understood;
Through aluminum,
steal;
Slotted bar event,
bent;
Inside screw,
you, two.

Design Studio Tad
Tokyo
Tadao Shimizu

New materials give a feeling of excitement because of their quality of freshness. However, just because something is new does not necessarily imply that it is good. Materials are a way of linking the past and future, in the same way that individuals do. What is important in this bonding is preserving and expressing the past while simultaneously expressing hope and dreams for the future.

In my materials I have used one of Japan's traditional techniques in the treatment of gold and silver (which only a few craftsmen in Kyoto continue to use) combined with a newly developed technique in the usage of this material. This immensely delicate material can be used for regular wallpaper, and I am thinking of using it for decorative shelves and in hotels and restaurants.

Ordieg Asociados
Barcelona
Gabriel Ordieg Cole

The different materials I have selected are the following:

Stone: A natural element, also related to the idea itself of building.

Corrugated aluminum sheet: An advanced technology material, with a texture which makes it visually exciting.

Silkscreened glass: Relates to graphic design, or to graphic elements in interior design. The motif in this particular case is taken from old floor tile designs common in Catalonia at the turn of the century.

Perforated board: Synthetic textured wood.

I believe that in the next few years the mixture of materials (traditional and high-tech, organic and non-organic) will be common in interior design, or in the built environment as a whole. And yet I also think that there is a difficult but necessary balance between materials which must be sought in order to avoid banality. Form and function. The way in which one achieves the mixture of different finishes, processes, or textures is one of the arts of building.

Larson Associates
Chicago

At Larson Associates we believe that texture and surface will be to the 1990s what color and form were to the 1960s. Whether this will be found in hard architectural materials or in soft, supple textiles, all will reflect an interest in the surface. New developments in manufacturing techniques will continue to inspire more innovative products. Also, there will be a demand for materials to look rich, yet cost little. We feel that this presentation, interweaving beautifully colored and constructed textiles and leather with stained wood, woven metal, and textured glass, reflects this direction for the future.

Trix and Robert Haussmann
Allgemeine Entwurfsanstalt
Zurich

We like the contrasts of these materials. We think that black is a beautiful non-color.

Kohn Pedersen Fox Conway Associates, Inc.
New York

Why did we select these materials?
Because of integrity, allusions to time . . . change, evolution, erosion, history, patina, fossils . . . and the gathering of available light.
of references to nature . . . paths, footprints, markings . . . and to craft . . . hands, tools, machines.
of contrasts . . . rough, smooth, flat, layered, soft, hard, warm, cold . . . and the dialogue of textures . . . and of their ability to comfort our senses.

Studio 80
Tokyo
Ikuyo Mitsuhashi

I try to realize my idea (image) with whatever materials can make it possible. Therefore, the black granite, various tiles, and colored concrete with pebbles are selected for this panel in order to realize the image I have.

I desire to create some kind of stream on the surface, so I have intentionally selected the various colored concrete with pebbles. That is to say, this various concrete is hand chiseled by skilled artisans who can create numbers of interesting textures by placing the chisel at certain angles.

dePolo/Dunbar Inc.
New York

At this time in history, we see the built environment being increasingly responsive to the concerns of global care, social issues, economic constraints, and consumer orientation. We expect to use both natural and manufactured materials with an emphasis on the latter. In addressing this prospect, we foresee greater manipulation of surface, having unexpected textures and colors inspired by a vast repertoire of chemical dyes and manufacturing processes. We expect that the modernist disciplines will be the armature upon which all of this is supported.

We approach the environment by exploring palettes of color, texture, and finishes that reflect attitudes about specific kinds of spaces. Our explorations in collage are inspired by an openness to the world around us, which helps to free us from being restricted by what is readily available in the marketplace. The collage has proven to be an easily understood form of communication.

Vicente Wolf Associates, Inc.
New York
Vicente Wolf

In the last year I have felt a strong pull toward more earth-orientated colors, and I have been getting away from stark white unapproachable spaces. When warm, elegant, luxurious, and functional elements are combined they create a comfortable and inviting environment.

Adam D. Tihany International Ltd.
New York

The deteriorating condition of our environment, the rapid destruction of nature, and the extinction of natural resources will force us to spend our time and funds in trying to preserve, restore, and imitate the glorious materials of the past: wood, marble, natural fabrics, and metals.

In the center of the panel, the reflection of the only material that can make the difference: you.

Bentley LaRosa Salasky, Architects and Decorators
New York

Materials can be common or exotic, an ageless class or a new invention. It is only in the application, the rendition, or the combination that we discover their extraordinary resonances.

Lembo Bohn Design Associates, Inc.
New York

We see a trend toward materials that evoke tranquility and have a strong connection to nature. By combining contrasting design elements—rusted metal, leaf-patterned wallpaper, silk velvet, rough-cut cedar—we have created a sophisticated yet whimsical composition.

Sussman/Prejza & Co.
Culver City, California

We have an affinity for materials that endure, both in their physical properties and in their classic qualities, and we take a special interest in combining them in novel ways—the precious with the common, the surprising color on the traditional surface.

A thoughtful attitude toward materialism is called for, one which values the treasures that surround us and move us to utilize our resources rather than to squander them. Within this framework lies ample room for delight.

Harry Teague Architects
Aspen, Colorado

The contradictory processes of mechanization and disintegration are melded together, forming a kind of suspended "terrazzo" of simple and sophisticated materials and techniques.

Rosenberg Kolb Architects
New York

As much as formal and spatial manipulation is the means of expressing design theory so too are the colors, textures, patterns, and composition of the materials used. Our work seeks to rethink the use of familiar materials, to use new materials in innovative ways. Our presentation is about contrasts: rough vs. smooth, dark vs. light, primitive vs. high-tech, man-made vs. natural, solid vs. broken, transparent vs. opaque. These are employed to articulate feelings and design concepts.

Johnson Fain and Pereira Associates
Los Angeles
R. Scott Johnson

Our collage defines a dialectic about the future of building materials. Two different trends will emerge, each charged by the same view of the future. Increasingly efficient means will generate a world of higher yields as well as a reinvigorated enthusiasm for mannerist expression.

One side of the dialectic is represented by our birch grid. The preeminence of the orthogonal in large-scale building will continue its emphasis on vertical standardization. Derived from their use in the nineteenth century as covering, these skins, or membranes, will derive their visual character again by the definitive properties of their technologies, much as the birch itself.

The other side of our dialectic is represented here by the heap of domestic fragments. While the membrane grids and their materials will be accessible to increasingly specialized groups, the proliferation of cheap, adaptive, and largely man-made materials will indulge the vanities of more broadly educated members in an increasingly mobile, informed society.

Fumio Shimizu Architects
Tokyo
Fumio Shimizu

Vertical Garden

My panel expresses a poetic message with architectural vocabulary. This is represented by the depth of the wall, voids, a combination of verticality and horizontality, and worn materials, juxtaposing wood and metal.

Evanson Studios
New York
James Evanson

My panel explores the relationship between the cold hardness of materials and the warm softness of light. The hand-rubbed surface of graphite into lacquer represents the artist's touch.

To combine art and utility is the objective.

To use black and white is not the objective.

To use gray only is not the goal.

To make simple is not the objective.

To express one definite thought is not the message.

To transform complexities of ideas into forms is the objective.

To combine the abstract and concrete is the goal.

Godley-Schwan
Brooklyn, New York

We have chosen materials that we feel are dominant in design now, such as mixtures of metals and wood, glass, stone and rubber. We feel an honesty emerging about the use of materials, employing the inherent qualities of natural materials and a mixture of soft and hard materials to create a more balanced feeling than apparent in the 1980s.

Design Partnership
San Francisco
Andrew Belschner, Joseph Vincent

We have limited our choices for *Mondo Materialis* to four. Each has a set of characteristics that we like, and each is distinctive yet compatible with other materials. Two are "natural" materials (oriented strand board [OSB], full top-grain leather), and two are "synthetic" (plastic laminate, galvanized metal). Two are "common" (OSB, galvanized metal), and the other two can be regarded as "fine" materials (leather, plastic laminate). Looked at another way, two are "finished"

(OSB: bleached, sanded, and sealed; galvanized metal: creased, sealed), and two have not had further treatment at our hands (high-gloss plastic laminate, aniline-dyed leather). Together, we feel these four examples represent a cross section of materials that we intend to use into the 1990s, embodying contrasting characteristics that allow imaginative juxtaposition.

Vignelli Associates
New York

In using materials we tend to create a memorable experience. Not through the use of expensive materials, but through the use of very simple materials, completely transformed by design. All materials reflect or absorb light according to their surface finish. Light is the master of form. It shapes the contours of an object, distinguishes hard surfaces versus those that are soft, transparent, or opaque.

We sense the importance of a viewer's perception and of articulate materials to achieve deliberate connotations, since whatever is perceived is retained and analyzed one way or another.

Lee H. Skolnick Architecture + Design
New York

One can use materials as signs; they are the basis of a language which accomplishes symbol and differentiation, inference and narration. In our syntax of materials we acknowledge the relative qualitative values ascribed to individual materials and reinterpret subjective principles regarding their use or combination. In the international cultural polyglot that characterizes the close of our century, the individualized regional languages of figurative decoration and ornamentation will give way to the more universal, evocative, and sensual language of compositions of natural and industrial-made materials.

The feel of wood.
The power of steel.
The timelessness of stone.

Ecco
New York
Eric Chan

The built environment in the next five years will be a juxtaposition of:

Soft touch
+
Hi-emotion
+
Hard and soft edges
+
Transparency
+
Semantics
+
Natural raw finishes
+
Depth, depth, and more depth

Briggs MacDonald
New York

I chose this combination of materials for their inherent beauty and variety of sensation, both tactile and visual. I see a trend begun in this decade and continuing into the next five years of an employment of combinations of natural materials (wood, granite) juxtaposed with manipulated "real" materials, glass, steel, metals, concrete, plaster. I see a disillusionment with synthetic materials and a finer honing of contrasts when different materials are employed together.

Drake & Boucher
New York
Robin Drake

I'm always shopping for new materials; sometimes I find them in the supermarket. (I rarely look in the architectural catalogues.) Occasionally I'm possessed with one color, and I'll take home anything if I like the color. Some of the best colors are on potato chip bags. I think there are some South American birds that collect anything blue. I'm a little like that bird.

Frederick Fisher Architect
Santa Monica, California

Material duality is the primary notion behind the selection of these materials: fragile/tough, light/heavy, natural/artificial, cheap/precious, transparent/massive, ancient/modern, subtle/garish.

The Moderns
New York

The Moderns seeks to push the envelope of contemporary design in an attempt to redefine the direction and content of modernism. This concept promotes the use of natural, innovative, and contrasting materials as a direction for architecture and design in the nineties. Tactile and warm, cool and functional—these concepts represent a shift in design culture from the pure logic of industry, i.e. rationalism, to the nature of society itself. The next industrial revolution requires the devising of soft and conceptual qualities that are more sophisticated and complex.

Boym Design Studio
New York
Constantin Boym

Selection of materials is a highly personalized matter, yet it inevitably reflects some general tendencies in design and architecture. In my choice I tried to capture new, emerging concepts, which might become prevalent in the upcoming decade:

1. It is an eclectic, all-inclusive collection of materials, high and low, expensive and throw away, which contrast, complement, and work off each other.
2. Materials and their combination have a slightly surreal edge such as the chance encounter of a sewing machine and an umbrella on a dissecting table as related to materials and surfaces.
3. Many materials look strange and unfamiliar, thus raising a question of doubt: "What is it?"
4. Jarring materials and colors lose their aggressive thrust, wild beasts of Memphis get domesticated, soft and user-friendly.
5. Simple, warm, banal materials, particularly wood and plywood, present an important reference point as they are related to idiosyncratic designers' materials.
6. Recycled materials and objects become a major ecological and cultural factor.

Anderson/Schwartz Architects
New York
Frederic Schwartz

Zora

"... Between each idea and each point of the itinerary an affinity or a contrast can be established, serving as an immediate aid to memory...."

Zora is a collage of conventional and nonconventional materials that are juxtaposed to establish a dialogue between the practical and the poetic. The materials have contrasting textures and appearances—hard versus soft, such as silk on hot-rolled steel, marble supported by 2 x 4s, and sheetrock. The subtext is illustrated by three Siamese fighting fish in Pyrex beakers on a shelf of Brazilian Blue marble.

> "...Zora's secret lies in the way your gaze runs over patterns following one another as in a musical score where one note can not be altered or displaced. The man who knows by heart how Zora is made, if he is unable to sleep at night can imagine he is walking along the streets and he remembers the order by which the copper clock follows the barber's striped awning, then the fountain with the nine jets, the astronomer's glass tower, the melon vendor's kiosk, the statue of the hermit and the lion, the Turkish bath, the café at the corner, the alley that leads to the harbor. Between each idea and each point of the itinerary an affinity or a contrast can be established, serving as an immediate aid to memory. So the world's most learned men are those who have memorized Zora..." (all text from Italo Calvino, *Invisible Cities,* p. 15)

John Lonczak Design
New York

Materials will be treated more preciously, artfully, and thoughtfully. A reclaimed reverence for each material and its properties will generate a new quality which is neither decadent nor stark. Never before has the time been more ripe for the appropriate use of material.

Robert W. Ebendorf
Santa Monica, California

I feel that in the next five years the artist, architect, and designer will be creating and designing more personal statements. The environment has become a social theater. The objects that we once took for granted are becoming a means for communication. These products and interior spaces display a sense of individualism and risk-taking. Colors, patterns, forms, textures, and most importantly, choice of materials can effectively counterbalance the plethora of microchip technology and standardized parts. In my way of thinking, there is little in terms of a unifying style or set philosophy of design. The main factor that brings these elements together—and sets them apart—is what they are made of or what they have or do not have in common.

As we move into the future, we will see an approach having more of a human touch (feeling, warmth, emotions, and risk-taking) by many creative designers, architects, and artists.

Franklin D. Israel Design Associates Inc.
Beverly Hills, California

Surreal Materiality

The materials of the future come from the imagination. They represent raw reality, yet demand that we as designers pay homage to what we ourselves have to give. Seeing the immediate world in different ways will help us select materials that best represent things as they are, and force us to understand better how precious are those things that protect us from that rawness and give us beauty, scale, and harmony. For it is that understanding which provides inspiration for the *new,* however shocking it might be.

Ivy Ross
Santa Monica, California

The next five years in the built environment will involve a process of un-building, chaos, instability, and asymmetry as a reflection of nature. It will be an exploration of the proper balance between nature and the built environment, an establishment of new relationships between man and nature and man and man. Time is a construction and nature one of the building blocks. Nothing is truly new anymore, we just see things differently. That must change. There is no longer one society, but many societies. Ways to express that individuality must be incorporated into the built environment. It must be able to grow and change just as individuals do over time. Those responsible must reach beyond short-term results for both the world within and the world around them. There is no longer one solution, but many questions. Why not?

Centro Design E Comunicazione s.r.l.
Milan
Francesco Binfarè

Concerning Art, Technology and the Ecological Problem

I see, in the near future, the use of materials that are natural when seminal, artificial when specific, complex and of high quality.

A collage: an opportunity to make a statement about an important theoretical issue.

The ecological problem is a problem of equilibrium. At the scientific level there is a great unbalance between technological understanding and intuitive conscience, meaning is the understanding of archetypal structures.

AD SA + Partners
Paris

In our hands we have the materials of the future. Innovation lies in the use and the mastering of new technologies. Architecture will find its everlasting character from the authenticity of materials and its renewal from the technologies applied.

Atelier de Pascal Mourgue
Paris

It is by considering the intelligent use of the materials of the past that we will create the materials of the future. Born from nature, they will be those that are produced and used intelligently. I do not know what the materials of the future will be, but every day I discover new ones.

Sam Lopata, Inc.
New York

Ideas, solutions, or design can be found in the unexpected. Let's share the magic of the object.

V. Kirpichev Association
Moscow, U.S.S.R.
Vladislav I. Kirpichev

Any material offers vast opportunities, awaiting utilization, new ideas. Together, materials and forms offer a richness to the designer of the future who is aware of the necessity of poetics and sensitivity to the environment. We must beware of reducing the goods found in our world into mere components for our workshops.

William Lipsey & Associates/Architects
Aspen, Colorado

Waves of information roll in and out.
This culture informs that culture
and vice versa.
We reach into the vast idea ocean
and hang our thoughts in the sun
for all to see and recycle.
In and out—again and again—
Drifting toward sameness.

The Challenge for the Nineties & Beyond:
How to use materials & forms in ways that
express our decreasing national
differences and yet maintain our
cultural uniqueness.

Dakota Jackson, Inc.
New York

MATERIALS + [CREATIVE] PROCESS
[TECHNICAL] PROCESS
[CULTURAL] PROCESS = [DESIGN]
EVOLUTION

Dakota Jackson, Inc., is expanding its seating collection, with leather as a key feature. In conjunction with Spinneybeck, we are developing a group of new leathers to be named /'lō-cus/:, which will forecast particular colors of interest to us. We are intrigued by the collision of traditional materials with innovative technologies and unorthodox approaches to design. The origami can be seen as a metaphor for unexpected processes by which materials can be manipulated, with the resulting product a surprising hybrid.

(/'lō-cus/:™ leathers are vegetable-tanned by a 19th century method exclusively for Dakota Jackson, Inc.)

Agnes Bourne, Inc.
San Francisco

The materials we have used are those in the furniture pieces manufactured for Agnes Bourne, Inc. They express a fresh, spontaneous exuberance, which characterizes the forty-one pieces in the collection, used in contract, hospitality, and residential application. Painted finishes, brightly colored simple woods, and woven leather combined with common materials such as wire glass, iron, found objects, and stencils produces an ecstatic assemblage for furniture products and environment.

Lewis and Mickle Studio
New York
Diane Lewis

I selected the images from *Mondo Cane,* a movie made in 1963 about the boundaries of civilization. Even highly refined construction systems and materials can be employed to perpetuate barbaric institutions. The refinement of materials does not lie in craft or technology, but in the intention and qualities of its author. The material challenge for the architect throughout history is to house the spirit.

Palette One *Acts and Substances*	*Palette Two* *Spirits and Qualities*
Rolled Mother-of-Pearl	Internal
Waxed Compacted Earth	Topography
Stamped Copper	Body
Milled Graphite	Distance
Embossed Plywood	
Forged Steel	Past
Wooden Terrazzo	
Warped Titanium	Vaultings
Polished Ivory	Matrix
Cast Glass	Muse
Printed Rubber	Mappings
Resined Felt	Womb
Perforated Stainless	
Fossilized Concrete	
Poured Lava	
Extruded Terra Cotta	
Coursed Brick	Present
Welded Steel	Fusion

Mary Little
London

As a determined and persistent designer of production furniture who has not yet succeeded in having a design put into large-scale production, I have chosen to introduce a selection of materials that I use for design development. My material resources comprise easily accessible, inexpensive materials that I use to build scale models or full-size mock-ups. By working in three dimensions from the early stages of the design program, I have the chance to develop a product mature in form, construction, composition. By using an ever-expanding base of materials for design development I can be more fluent in my design process, which touches and effects every design project.

Fitch RS
London

The theme of our panel is contradiction and prediction. Contradiction arises from the William Morris chintz design, "Tulips and Willow." Morris (1834–1896), medievalist, Romantic, and perhaps Britain's greatest designer, loathed the modernity of his contemporary world and mistrusted modern materials and values. He argued for a society that would turn away from mass production and return to the days of craftsmanship. Prediction is demonstrated by the inclusion of materials which suggest a return to Morris's values. The environmental crisis, growing consumer awareness and unrest, perhaps suggests a return to more natural materials and a more transparent design ethic.

Marie-Christine Dorner
Architecture Intérieure—Design
Paris
Marie-Christine Dorner

I love cheerful interiors. Architectural elements are more like potential friends, faithful and silent. One looks forward to meeting them again for their physical and visual comfort. More and more, they will take on the role of a layer of clothing, made of foam, or leather, or fabric, chosen with care for their functional qualities and for their wit and presence. Lightness will be an additional and necessary quality of these "movable objects"—furniture, of course, but also partitions, kitchens, bathrooms, which are less and less integrated into the architecture. This (architecture?) will develop toward its fundamental/primordial role of "shelter for objects."

Roger Kraft: Architecture • Design
Kansas City, Missouri
Roger Kraft

The literalness with which new or exotic materials can in themselves make a design statement is generally not a factor in my work. Rather, I prefer to select materials based upon their ability to reinforce and orchestrate larger formal hierarchies. And since it is these relationships that interest me most, my choice of materials is and will continue to be quite unpredictable, determined less by novelty or personal bias than by the requirements and possibilities of the project in question. Consequently, my response to the questions raised by this exhibition is less about the particular materials I may use next, but more of a statement about the attitudes that will govern their use.

In designing my panel for the "Mondo Materialis" exhibition, I was primarily interested in the manner in which various decorative, expressive, and spatial elements could be set into an otherwise inert plane to render it vital and plastic. My use of materials here is analogous to the use of materials in Cubist painting or in Italian Renaissance architecture, for example, in which the intrinsic value of a given material is less significant than its relative preciousness or richness within the overall material palette. The wood, glass, paper, drawing, and paint media used in my panel have been selected for their abilities to create a complementary set of formal and plastic incidents and points of emphasis within an overall structure and image. The orchestration transcends the materials, as I think it should in matters of art and culture.

The panel also reveals my current disenchantment with excessively technological ideas and a new delight in mythically evocative and poetically derived ones. Hopefully, the distortion of a potentially endless square grid is a symbol suggesting a bending of technical rationalism to the enhancement of the human realm; by this I do not mean to imply something loose or easy, but rather an endeavor requiring great focus and determination. The reciprocity of functionalism, poetry, and formal rigor within the work of Le Corbusier continues to be a model for me.

Finally, I wanted to reflect in my presentation my own involvement with painting, an interest which will no doubt continue to inform my work as an architect and designer.

Berthet-Pochy
Paris

The Materials of the 1990s

In the coming decade, two distinct kinds of forces will occupy front stage.

1. *Shadows and light*

On the one hand, light will be used as a material structuring space, molding volumes, giving life to a setting, creating new perspectives, different spaces, and dreams.

2. *Tradition and actuality*

On the other, there will be a definite return to natural (stone, wood, leather, wool) and traditional materials. It is not a question of a step backward, but rather of a harmony between a perfect knowledge of yesterday's materials and today's creativity.

To the interior designer and architect, the actuality of his conceptions is doubtless more important than the pseudo-modernism of "new materials." Why make a desk out of carbon fiber *[fibre de carbone]* when, except for its fashionable aspect, it will have nothing but drawbacks: high cost, and excessive lightness that will make it necessary to "ballast" the whole thing in order to make it serviceable.

Quality and permanence

Any contemporary setting requires the achievement of high quality: as in great cooking, the "basic ingredients" are decisive. The demand for quality and durability plays an integral role in the choice of materials, which also explains the return to natural and traditional materials.

Gere Kavanaugh/Designs
Los Angeles
Gere Kavanaugh

This photo-collage of materials, which comes from all over the world, is the wall in the back of my desk. It is my visual bank.

Paul Ludick
New York

These materials represent a simplicity of forms and densities. But within these basic materials and in combination with each other a communication occurs between materials and user. This communication is my work.

details
New York

The dream is a lie but the dreaming is true.
—Robert Penn Warren

Given our greater understanding of the structure of matter, an influx of new materials has revolutionized the way that we as designers must interpret technology and translate it into a new formal language for design. The Cubist-like image we have produced is symbolic of the potential impact that these materials hold in the world of form. Just as nearly a century ago Cubism shocked the world's preconceptions of composition, light, space, and time, these materials are creating a new frontier. We are entering the last decade of the twentieth century, and the feeling that the future has arrived is omnipresent. Novel material innovations are certain to be the very stuff upon which the future will be built.

fitch richardsonsmith +
Columbus, Ohio

Materials are deceiving!

GK Industrial Design Associates
Tokyo

Design Concept
The Ekuan Design Mandala

\+ *On the Expression Intent*

Kenju Ekuan scans the world from a global viewpoint. His stance is aimed at nothing more or less than discerning the heart of things, the people of the world, and the essence of design. The spirit of the Mandala ("Manda" meaning essence and "La" meaning to obtain) carves out a new age for design.

\+ *On the Expression Technology*

Kraft paper is attached to a kraft mat. "Material on Material." The expressive technique of receiving images from the material itself brings out a new interpretation of those materials.

The Burdick Group
San Francisco
Bruce Burdick

New materials and the techniques for using them produce the major breakthroughs we see in furniture design (think of Charles Eames's use of plywood and fiberglass). This is not to say that new materials alone generate significant design. It takes a prepared mind to exploit the opportunity within these materials; for example, both molded plywood and fiberglass had been applied to furniture previous to the Eames application. Because new materials are not created everyday, furniture innovation consists in utilizing given materials in new combinations or applications to meet existing or changing needs. This work is difficult and challenging. If one is not very careful, the only change is in fashion, not innovation.

Cesar Pelli & Associates Inc.
New York
Cesar Pelli

This is an extraordinary moment in architecture because we still have the intellectual inheritance of the architectural past, but we also have new products whose nature will allow us to create forms that are fresh and new. It is up to us to invent the ways to use them. Most exciting is how we explore the artistic qualities inherent in new products. Complexity and richness come from working within a living system of construction technology.

Studio Cini Boeri
Milan
Cini Boeri

Memories, hopes, and curiosities will follow me into the future. And when I shall no longer be in the world of living beings my spirit will float over materials and architecture with a critical insight that only then I will be able to express freely. Maybe I will see beautiful materials and architectures, but I will be unable to touch them with my hand. ("Mat" is the root of "material" and I was told that in Sanskrit it means "to touch with hand.")

I will see airplanes in the sky, invisible to everyone other than myself, because they, too, will be transparent. I will see glass reflecting light, replacing rooftops, in which not only people but also the sky and the sea will be mirrored. Maybe, even, I will see small architects walking beneath multilayer towns, trying to relate to their scale.

If those architects are free and rational beings, rather than slaves of images and powerful despots, then they will enjoy the possibility of choosing among natural materials historically passed along our profession. This also means they will be able to keep a critical distance from manufactured materials, offered to us by today's market. Artificial materials will be subject to continuous transformations, signs of technological progress which will become the proof of our civilization's achievements.

But if I shall be still alive, then I will be able not only to see but also to touch with my hand the soft surface of wood, the roughness of stone, the freezing metals. I will also passionately mold new plastic materials, cutting them with lasers to get the exact size and shape the project demands; I will enjoy the warmth and coolness of thermal fabrics; I will draw with optical fibers on three-dimensional grids.

But, most important, I will enjoy molding, with the help of sophisticated technologies, the material I like best—glass, with its reflections, thickness, sizes, curves, and edges. I will use it extensively in my projects, remembering Frank Lloyd Wright's timeless lesson: to always work "in the nature of materials."

Community Redevelopment Agency
Los Angeles
John Kaliski

Mondo Materialis (what is needed to get the job done in the 90s (and beyond . . .)

Attitude	Asphalt
Bodily fluids	Bait
Chaos	Credit
Dreams	Dynamite
Electromagnetism	Elastic
Fate	Files
Grist for the mill	Gilt
History	Hard knocks
Intuition	Institutions
Jaywalking	Junk mail
Knots	Kryptonite
Law	Liquid Plumber
Means	Moonbeams
Osmosis	Oatmeal
Problems	Publicity
Questions	Quarks
Risk	Rights
Semiotics	Shit
Tendencies	Therapy
Urges	U-turns
Violence	Velcro
Wishes	Water soluble
X-rated	Xerography
You as well as me	Yen
Zeitgeist	Zoning

Hardy Holzman Pfeiffer Associates
New York
Hugh Hardy

Quality building requires a sure sense of materials. The differences between stone and sheetrock, plaster and polyvinyl, steel and glass are essential to realizing fine architecture. Whether buildings are built for profit or aesthetic merit, have lavish or modest budgets, their architects must recognize the value of effectively using materials so that buildings can respond to contemporary needs. The ornamental richness of traditional buildings is appealing, but contemporary designs can use different methods and sensibilities to achieve the same results. A fearless use of the vast array of new materials now available is both desirable and within our grasp.

Kalil Studio
New York
Michael Kalil

When we first appeared beyond the edge of our world and from the silence of space looked back toward earth, we could only imagine a fraction of the changes in store for us. The technology that made a place for us in a starry universe has transformed our ideas about citizenship, redefined our relationship to place, and totally changed the architectural materials of the industrial age. With the arrival of the electronic age, an individual's relationship to place is no longer confined to a specific point on the earth. Our boundaries are not the edges of nations but the limitless space of our universe. This shift in the scale of place has also redefined our scale of the city. Our cities are no longer made of skyscrapers, but are a constant flow of energy and information which structures our new architecture.

The architecture of our familiar cities is made from the unyielding dominant materials of the industrial age. It is an architecture (built to an international aesthetic) that applies the same rigorous materials and structures to all the societies and climates of the world. Yet the materials that established us in the universe bring an entirely new paradigm to our relationship to place. They are responsive and they can process information from the environment, such as brightness and temperature, and adjust to suit our specific needs.

These materials have also expanded our cities. Cities, as we now know them, are rooms in the greater universal city. Telephone lines serve as our doors, electromagnetic waves are our windows. With the new materials created during the space age, place takes on the characteristics of ourselves and our environment.

Space has revealed to us a universe so beautiful and so full of surprises that even our imagination could not have constructed it. But in opening the earth outward to this much larger sphere, we have stretched the ingenuity of our materials, creating capabilities we had not previously seen a need for. Their flexibility has opened up the universe and increased our awareness of the potentials on earth. We have again learned a lesson from the harmony of the spheres and brought ourselves closer to the heavens.

Legorreta Arquitectos
California/Mexico
Ricardo Legorreta

Design is the combination
of imagination
and materials
imagination is a human quality
materials are the result
of either
God's or man's creation
the challenge
of the designer
is to use his imagination
and take advantage
of the enormous variety
of materials offered by
that of the contemporary civilization
I hope
we respond to it

Alessandro Mendini
Milan

Artificial Materials

There is a great conceptual—perhaps even ideological—difference between natural materials (iron, fired clay, wood, etc.) and synthetic (or plastic or ambiguous or "unnatural") materials. In fact, the competition between the materials that nature provides directly, and the new materials that are custom-made precisely to the requirements of specific objects, calls into question the very principles and rules of design.

The new identity of materials, their total transformation and silent revolution, changes our cultural approach to the world of objects completely. The materials of the past, with their great tradition, had powerful identities; in the course of the radical shift in the idea of materials, "identity" has been replaced by its opposite: the new materials are, indeed, without identity. They are malleable, ready for anything, a continuum of infinite possibilities.

Today's designer freely imagines the material before imagining the object. Once upon a time, however, the artisan forced his object's shape into the rigid rules of a particular, pre-existing material.

Where is the ideological leap? It resides in the fact that the natural world no longer exists, that the world has become entirely artificial. Forest, sea, and sky are distant, uninteresting fancies. Our real "naturalness" consists in our methodical, progressive distancing of ourselves from nature. Clean air, real food, undeveloped landscapes pain us moderns, the "sentimental robots." We don't like them, nor do we know how to use them. The boundaries between real and false have vanished, everything has become make-believe; people and things are like mirror-images or souvenirs of themselves. In this context, *plastic* becomes the perfect, multiform material to resolve our need for ambiguity and simulation. Plastic—the word itself tells it—is so without identity as to have, on the contrary, an infinite number of identities. It allows us to say that "today, any image is possible."

Imitation leather, imitation wood, imitation silk, imitation marble, imitation crocodile or tortoiseshell—there is no more inviting adventure for a designer than to reject the classical concept of inspiration, and sink into the use of this visionary, elusive, caramel-like material that varies from solid to liquid to transparent. Even the "wax" figure of the wax museum has been replaced by a hyperrealistic "plastic" figure, more lifelike than the original. And contrariwise, if traditional materials are to enjoy a second childhood today, if they are to be new and still credible, they must look fake. Leather is pressed, polished, and dyed; it is worthwhile only if it looks like plastic. Wood is ground up and re-formed to be synthetic and different from itself. Marble is sliced into the thinnest sheets and used as if it were a light laminate. Everything real must lose the odor of nature, must be dipped in neutrality, accept that its singularity will become promiscuous, on pain of falling into oblivion. Aldo Rossi designs a table made of marble, but it looks like a traditional old wooden table. Robert Haussmann designs a soft fabric that looks like marble. A thing is real if it looks fake, and is fake if it looks real. With synthetic materials, even species multiply: (mass-produced) artificial flowers don't just look like carnations, roses, and daisies; they become whole new families—more complex, more colorful, and more expressive. The idea is to supplant, to outdo nature's imagination.

This, then, is the mirage of today's designer: to turn the whole world, the whole house even, not so much into gold, as into plastic. And what happens? In reaction to this extreme need, there burgeons within the Post-modern breast the opposite need: to scratch the dirt with our nails, in search of real dirt, a deeply anthropological necessity for an archaic return to our origins, to the untamed forest. In the cruel and violent computerized urban forest, the sentimental robot seeks to stand out. No more things made only out of plastic, no more mass ideas, no more assembly-line objects repeated ad infinitum, each one identical to the one before—instead, diversity, ritualism, eclecticism. And with this reversal, this gaze toward distant shapes, plastic itself, this youthful, agnostic material, undergoes an identity crisis of its very own.

Studio Citterio
Milan
Antonio Citterio, Terry Dwan

As we create architecture in an age of uncertainty, we find ourselves to be uninhibited and anxious. We tend toward a design rigor that incorporates form and symbol through the use of materials and new technologies. Today, the term high-tech has come to refer primarily to the preceding two decades of a particular arrangement of structural and building materials and services. We would rather not be labeled this way, but would prefer instead to be known as "engineer-philosophers." We try to give life to the representation of structure, to formalize connections, and to illuminate construction details. We work hard to avoid creating delusions, unfulfilled promises, symbols without meaning. As Eileen Gray states: "Every work of art is a symbol. There is no need to go back to the excessive decoration of the past... sometimes it is enough just to choose an object which is in itself beautiful material." Certainly the use of selected materials immediately calls to mind past epochs, some more recent, some more distant in time. But as in the case of zinced steel, the actual procedural design rigor, or the beauty of the finishing itself, can transcend the referential allusions of the material. A historical perspective aids in overcoming design limitations of either the high-tech style of the sixties or the beginning of the industrial revolution. Our work is low-tech, we are artisans and architects. As Modernists, we try to sensitively, aesthetically, resolve functional problems using any of numerous materials available: scale, detail, humor.

Tigerman McCurry Architects
Chicago
Stanley Tigerman

Does your work have a moral significance?

I believe that the theory informing my current architectural production, a theory I have come to call "failed attempts at healing an irreparable wound," has moral significance. Through my recent projects I have expressed my concern that the ethical imperative of architecture be fulfilled. Etymologically, architecture is about existence, about being in a state of peace. There is something ultimately hopeful about that proposition, even when viewed in the context of contemporary cultural disjunctions. To employ design strategies based on dislocation alone is not a valid approach, for it denies the essential optimism of the human spirit; but neither can we seek verification through historicism. As architects, we must search within ourselves for ennobling possibilities in an attempt to redress the flaws, or wounds, that we acknowledge to be unique to our era. An architecture emanating from such concerns becomes a poignant embodiment of values that replenish the human spirit. Our ability to remain optimistic in the face of otherwise ominous visions represents the tempering of hope with pragmatism. The very quest for such possibilities is a healing one, and indicates an awakening to the pluralistic needs of contemporary society and the necessity of reconciling them through architectural expression. I am deeply committed to this quest, both in my writing and in my projects.

Venturi, Rauch, Scott-Brown
Philadelphia
Robert Venturi

Faux is Ok

It is hard to discuss the issue of new materials in the environment because we no longer have an aesthetic that promotes what Frank Lloyd Wright called "the nature of materials," one of the main ideas on which modern design was based. We then gloried in the explicit expression of materials old and new; Le Corbusier's poured concrete as Béton Brut is an example of the latter. When Wright as a young designer realized that Louis Sullivan's ornament did not connect with the nature of materials, new or old, and that Sullivan's ornament was the same in its relief, whether it was in terra cotta, brick, or iron, he discovered that he had gone beyond his master. I must say I had a similar feeling of elation when I realized conversely that the nature of materials does not essentially matter as a matter of aesthetics—that kind of harmony, or easy unity, was out.

Why? Perhaps we are simply no longer as thrilled by new materials and advanced technology but accept the innovations as a matter of course. Or maybe it is just that our aesthetic is less materially and formally based and more symbolically based. Symbolism, association, and reference to historical or at least non-material-technical-structural-formal characteristics matter less, or rather, referential symbolic elements (which Modernism disdained) matter more.

So sometimes, in truly mannerist ways, we enjoy going against the nature of the material or structure. We glory in the contradiction between form and material in order to promote symbol. When carried to the extreme, this approach involves a tour de force. Sometimes looks and material don't go together. So what!? We now say we enjoy the contradiction. That's life—when what you say and what you do don't necessarily fit easily. Faux is *ok*.

List of Contributors

A + O Studio
San Francisco

ABLE
New York

AD SA + Partners
Paris

Adam D. Tihany International Ltd.
New York

Agnes Bourne, Inc.
San Francisco

Alessandro Mendini
Milan

Anderson/Schwartz Architects
New York

Andrea Branzi Architetto
Milan

Arquitectonica International Corporation
Coral Gables, Florida

Artorium Inc.
Montreal, Quebec

Associates & Ferren
Wainscott, New York

Atelier de Pascal Mourgue
Paris

Bentley LaRosa Salasky,
Architects and Decorators
New York

Berthet-Pochy
Paris

Boym Design Studio
New York

Briggs MacDonald
New York

The Burdick Group
San Francisco

Casson Mann Designers
London

CDM Castelli Design Milano s.r.l
Milan

Centro Design E Comunicazione s.r.l.
Milan

Cesar Pelli & Associates Inc.
New York

Community Redevelopment Agency
Los Angeles

Coop Himmelblau Vienna/Los Angeles
West Los Angeles

Dakota Jackson, Inc.
New York

Dan Chelsea Design
New York

Danny Lane
London

David Zelman
New York

Denis Santachiara
Milan

Dennis Oppenheim
New York

dePolo/Dunbar Inc.
New York

Design Partnership
San Francisco

Design Studio Tad
Tokyo

details
New York

Donald Kaufman Color
New York

Donovan and Green
New York

Drake & Boucher
New York

Ecart SA
Paris

Ecco
New York

Eric Owen Moss—Architect
Culver City, California

Eva Jiricna Architects
London

Evanson Studios
New York

fitch richardsonsmith +
Columbus, Ohio

Fitch RS
London

Franklin D. Israel Design Associates Inc.
Beverly Hills, California

Frederick Fisher Architect
Santa Monica, California

FTL Associates
New York

Fumio Shimizu Architects
Tokyo

Gere Kavanaugh/Designs
Los Angeles

GK Industrial Design Associates
Tokyo

Godley-Schwan
Brooklyn, New York

Haigh Space Architects/Designers
Greenwich, Connecticut

Hardy Holzman Pfeiffer Associates
New York

Harry Teague Architects
Aspen, Colorado

Herbert Pfeifer
San Jose, California

ID TWO
San Francisco

Ivy Ross
Santa Monica, California

James Hong Design
New York

Jeffrey Beers Architects
New York

John Lonczak Design
New York

Johnson Fain and Pereira Associates
Los Angeles

Jonathan R. W. Teasdale
New York

Kalil Studio
New York

Kallmann McKinnell & Wood
Architects, Inc.
Boston

Kawakami Design Room
Tokyo

King-Miranda Associati
Milan

Kohn Pederson Fox Conway
Associates, Inc.
New York

Kozo Design Studio Inc.
Tokyo

Larson Associates
Chicago

Lee H. Skolnick
Architecture + Design
New York

Legorreta Arquitectos
California/Mexico

Lembo Bohn Design Associates, Inc.
New York

Lewis & Mickle Studio
New York

McCoy & McCoy
Bloomfield Hills, Michigan

Marie-Christine Dorner
Architecture intérieure—Design
Paris

Martine Bedin
Milan

Mary Little
London

Masayuki Kurokawa Architect
& Associates
Tokyo

Metropolitan Furniture Corporation
South San Francisco

Michael McDonough, Architect
New York

Michael Sorkin
New York

The Moderns
New York

Murphy/Jahn
Chicago

M. W. Steele Group, Inc.
San Diego

Nanda Vigo
Milan

Nederlandse Philips Bedrijven B.V.
Eindhoven, The Netherlands

nob + non
New York

Ordieg Asociados
Barcelona

Orlando Diaz-Azcuy Designs
San Francisco

Padrós/Riart/Tió Mobles Casas
Barcelona

Paolo Portoghesi ed Associati
Rome

Paul Ludick
New York

Pei, Cobb, Freed & Partners
New York

Peter Marino & Associate Architects
New York

Peter Stathis/Scott Zukowski
New York/Indianapolis

PHH Environments
Los Angeles

Pui-Pui Li & Eric Jones
Staten Island, New York

Ricardo Bofill
Taller de Arquitectura
Paris

Richard Meier & Partners
Los Angeles/New York

The Richard Penney Group
New York

Robert W. Ebendorf
Santa Monica, California

Roger Kraft: Architect • Design
Kansas City, Missouri

Rogers and Goffigon Ltd.
Greenwich, Connecticut

Rosenberg Kolb Architects
New York

Ross Lovegrove
London

Sam Lopata, Inc.
New York

Smart Design, Inc.
New York

Sottsass Associati
Milan

Steelcase Inc.
Grand Rapids, Michigan

Studio Cini Boeri
Milan

Studio Citterio
Milan

Studio De Lucchi
Milan

Studio 80
Tokyo

Studio Nurmesniemi Ky
Helsinki

Studio Sowden
Milan

Sumform
Long Island City, New York

Sussman/Prejza & Co.
Culver City, California

Syndesis, Inc.
Santa Monica, California

Thun Design
Milan

Tigerman McCurry Architects
Chicago

Tom McHugh
Philadelphia

Torck-Noirot
Paris

Torsten A. Fritze
San Francisco

Trix and Robert Haussmann
Allgemeine Entwurfsanstalt
Zurich

Vanderbyl Design
San Francisco

V. Kirpichev Association
Moscow

Vent Design Associates
Campbell, California

Venturi, Rauch, Scott-Brown
Philadelphia

Vicente Wolf Associates, Inc.
New York

Vignelli Associates
New York

Walz Design
New York

Weber & Kalmes
Luxembourg

The Whitney Group, Inc.
Houston, Texas

William Lipsey & Associates/Architects
Aspen, Colorado

William McDonough Architects
New York

Wood/Marsh
East Melbourne, Australia

Zebra Design Inc.
New York

Curated Materials

ALPIPARQ®
Alpi SpA
Modigliana, Italy 47015

CELLULOSE ACETATE
Delmar Products
Berlin, Connecticut 06037

COLDECOR
Akzo Coatings Inc.
Montclair, New Jersey 07042

CORE PINE PARTICLE BOARD WITH
CUSTOM APPLIED FINISH
Boise Cascade
Boise, Idaho 83728–0001

CUSTOM TERRAZZO (IN TILE FORM)
Wausau Tiles
Wausau, Wisconsin 54402

DICHROIC GLASS
Associates & Ferren
Wainscott, New York 11975

DRYVIT OUTSULATION®
(RUSTOLEUM SILVER PAINT)
Dryvit
West Warwick, Rhode Island 02893

ELECTROLUMINESCENT LAMP
Nichia Chemical Industry
Tokyo, Japan 108

GLUE CHIP GLASS
American Scene
Chicago, Illinois 60606

HAND-WOVEN BAUXITE
Silk Dynasty
Mountain View, California 94039

IRIDESCENT GLASS
S. A. Bendheim & Co.
New York, New York 10013

IRIDESCENT & INTERFERENCE
ACRYLICS
Golden Artist Colors Inc.
New Berlin, New York 13411

KEVLAR
CARBON FIBER CLOTH
Mutual Industries Inc.
Philadelphia, Pennsylvania 19120

REBOND CARPET UNDERLAYMENT
Steve's Custom Floor Covering
Buena Vista, Colorado 81211

RUBBER TILE (GOM-TB)
Fuso Gum Industry Co., Ltd.
Saitama-Ken, Japan

SUPER-CUSHION®
INTERLOCKING MATTING
#SC1081
American Floor Products Inc.
Rockville, Maryland 20850

SYNDECRETE
Syndesis
Santa Monica, California 90404

SYNTAL
Smorgan Industries
Ermington, N.W.W.,
2115 Australia

WAFER OR ORIENTED
STRAND BOARD
Georgia Pacific
Atlanta, Georgia 30348

Acknowledgments

Mondo Materialis was an exhibition based on a concept by Jeffrey J. Osborne. It was curated by George M. Beylerian and Jeffrey J. Osborne.

Special thanks to Ruth Lande Shuman for working tirelessly on the exhibition and for coordinating the information in this book. Thanks to Paul Haigh for giving us the title *Mondo Materialis*.

Very special gratitude to our friends at Harry N. Abrams, Inc.—To Paul Gottlieb for his enthusiasm about this project; to Ruth Peltason for her endless patience in editing the inordinate amount of material from 125 participants, and for streamlining the content and the format; and to Sam Antupit for his masterful treatment and art direction of this exciting material.

And 125 thanks to all the participants whose contributions made this work possible.